HOW TO MAKE MONEY IN COMMODITIES:

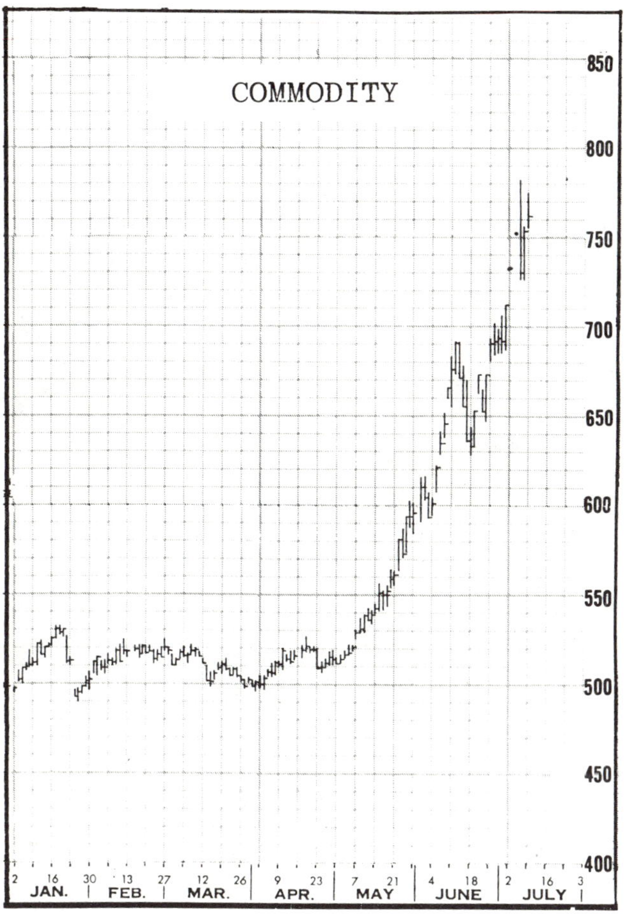

The Successful Method For Today's Markets

by

Dr. Bruce G. Gould

Second Edition, Revised.
 Additional copies available from BRUCE GOULD PUBLICATIONS, P.O. Box 16, Seattle, WA 98111.

(ISBN 0-918706-05-9)

CONTENTS

PREFACE

The business of commodity futures trading grew spectacularly throughout the 1970s and into the present decade. The value of commodities traded on the futures exchanges zoomed past the $2.5 **trillion** mark, dwarfing similar statistics for the New York Stock Exchange. The volume of trading in commodity futures set new records **every single year** from 1969-1980, racking up a 700 percent increase to nearly 80 million contracts (the unit bought or sold in futures trading). Clearly, thousands of investors had discovered the enormous profit opportunites in soybeans, wheat, gold, cotton, sugar, Treasury Bills, hogs and cattle. In fact, most of the 40 major commodities traded on the U.S. exchanges offered at some time returns of 100 percent or more on initial capital. Many, as this book will detail, brought astonishing profits of **3,000 or 4,000 percent** of the original outlay.

As is evident from the many actual case histories this book will examine, such profits are not unusual in commodities, nor are they reserved for an elite group of professionals. They occur frequently, and can be had by any trader with the method for spotting a certain kind of trend and properly capitalizing on it. The tremendous growth of the futures industry testifies to the fact that many average investors have found trading in commodity futures easier, more exciting, and more lucrative than investment in stocks, bonds, or other conventional instruments. These latter are essential to any sound investment program, but none can bring the returns, personal and financial, of futures trading. Unfortunately, many who flocked to the commodity markets suffered ruinous losses. These might have been avoided by the disciplined use of a single, simple approach to profiting through price changes.

This book is **not** a complete guide to futures trading (a task I have attempted elsewhere). It is instead a brief introduction, and a handbook for developing one successful trading method. Commodity futures trading has been my life for the past 15 years. I began trading futures contracts while still a student in law school. Since then I have never ceased following the markets, for commodity profits are indeed gratifying. My career as a trader has convinced me that futures trading is a practical alternative for people from all walks of life — farmers, retailers, professionals, homemakers — who seek to increase their earnings.

Commodity futures trading has been shrouded in a darkness of misinformation until quite recently. Many still believe it to be a hopelessly complicated and dangerous enterprise. I have tried to fill that information gap in my best-selling *Dow Jones-Irwin Guide To Commodities Trading,* and to give concrete answers to traders' questions in my *Commodity Trading Manual* and in a bi-weekly newsletter, "Bruce Gould on Commodities." But my regular correspondence with traders — from beginners to seasoned professionals — still brings one insistent question: "Bruce, what really is the most successful technique you have developed for making money in the futures markets?" In the last 15 years I have tested a score of systems, and researched dozens more. My own time and money were spent in these efforts, testing different market strategies with my own risk capital. Out of these efforts came the answer to the question so many keep asking. This book presents that answer in a case-by-case review of actual price moves in the recent past that offered stunning profits when traded with the method you are about to learn.

This revelation should have two major effects. First, a great number of people should make a large sum of money as a result of carefully reading the following pages. You may well be one of them, and I hope that you are. Second, my answer to the posed question will undoubtedly upset a small group of professional "insiders" who have kept the secrets of successful trading to themselves in the past, and who would like to keep making money from the ignorance of the investing public. This book and my other writings are designed to change that situation forever.

You will probably be amazed by what you are about to learn. You may even be frightened. Certainly you will be suspicious and unbelieving at first (as you should be concerning **any** investment opportunity). But the argument is a true one, and the facts speak for themselves. It is possible to make profits in the commodity futures markets running from 100 percent to 500 percent to more than 5,000 percent in a matter of weeks or months, and with an initial risk capital outlay of as little as $5,000. I have done it, and it is being done today **on a regular basis** by many traders. In small towns and big cities, on farms and in offices, traders with no expertise in crop forecasting or hog-corn ratios are making very healthy fortunes by patiently applying a simple approach to the movements of the markets.

Upon completion of these pages, however, I **do not** suggest that you borrow money from the bank or cash in your life insurance policy in order to get started in commodities. Remember, the vast majority of traders lose money, mostly because of greed, impatience, and a lack of common sense. Many rush haphazardly into markets, trading fast and furious on the basis of rumors and intuitions, or according to some high-priced and "sure fire" system. The commission costs alone on all these trades are often enough to break the novice trader. I urge you to **start very slowly.** Commit only a small amount of money that you can comfortably afford to risk. Better yet, begin by trading only "on paper," keeping your money in the bank while conducting your paper trading exactly as if it were the real thing. Get a feel for how to spot a profitable trading opportunity, and develop the timing essential for getting in and out of your positions with maximum efficiency. Once you've mastered the technique on paper, and are showing consistent net profits, you are ready to join the ranks of the winning speculators.

Good reading and good luck!

Bruce Gould
Seattle, Washington

ACKNOWLEDGEMENTS

First, I would like to thank the thousands who made the first edition of this book such a gratifying success. Their letters and comments have made a valuable contribution to my further studies of the futures markets, and deepened immeasurably my understanding of the average trader's needs.

I would like to dedicate this book to several very important people in my life, Fred, Doreen and Peter Pomeroy, David and Jan Gould, Harvey and Sally Cupaiuloi, Christine McComb, and the most wonderful mother a son could have, Grace Elizabeth Gould.

Note: All commodity price charts reproduced in this book are courtesy of the Commodity Research Bureau, Inc., 1 Liberty Plaza, New York, New York 10006.

SECTION ONE

DEFINITIONS AND BASIC PRINCIPLES

I

What are "commodities"? What goes on at a "commodity futures exchange"? How can one beat the high cost of living by buying and selling "futures contracts"? Answering these basic questions is the purpose of this book. By the time you are done, you should be well on your way to understanding how to **profit from inflations and recessions** with a moderate investment of risk capital (money you can easily afford to lose). Commodity futures trading is a fast-paced game of speculation, wherein traders try to guess whether the price of a commodity will go up or down. The attraction of the game is that profits come no matter which way prices go, as long as the trader has gotten on the right side of the market before the big price move travels very far. For a relatively small amount of deposit money (called "margin"), the trader controls the contractual rights to deliver or accept, at some set date in the future, large quantities of goods (corn, silver, cocoa, Treasury Bonds, etc.). The trader thus profits or loses as the price of the commodity changes during the time the contract is held. The relatively small margin as compared to the value of the contract means that profits, and losses, can be many times greater than the amount of money initially invested. Best of all, the contract so held can be traded away (and profits or losses realized) long before the delivery date, so that no actual goods are ever physically involved.

But now let's start at the beginning, with the very word "commodities." The dictionary defines "commodity" as "something of use, advantage, or value. . . . an article of trade or commerce, especially a product as distinguished from a service." These abstractions hide the fact that commodities are an essential part of everyone's daily life. When we go to the supermarket, department store, bank or auto showroom, we go into the commodities business. The shock of prices that seem never to go down reflects a keen awareness of commodity prices and their fluctuations. In such painful moments, we know what commodities are: beef, pork, chicken, eggs, potatoes, coffee, cereals, salad oil, sugar, et. al. These are, as the dictionary said, things "of use, advantage, or value." They are also all commodities that can be traded on a futures exchange. A look about you will speedily discover more commodities in your life. Is there cotton in your shirt or dress? Was your house built with plywood or lumber? Did you take out a mortgage to finance it? Does your jewelery contain silver or gold? Have you borrowed money from the bank lately, or invested in government securities? In every case you were involved in a commodity transaction, and in every case that commodity could be found on one of the U.S. futures exchanges.

We live in a world of commodities. Our material lives are nothing more or less than the organized process of producing and distributing commodities. In the world of commodities, there is a continual fluctuation between excess supply and desperate scarcity. Those fluctuations translate into the roller coaster ride of commodity prices. One year gasoline sells for 30 cents a gallon; the next year 60 cents; the next year $1.25, and so on. A bumper crop of wheat drives the price per bushel down to $1.50. Then huge orders from the Soviet Union send prices to $6.00. Then the reverse occurs and prices plummet a

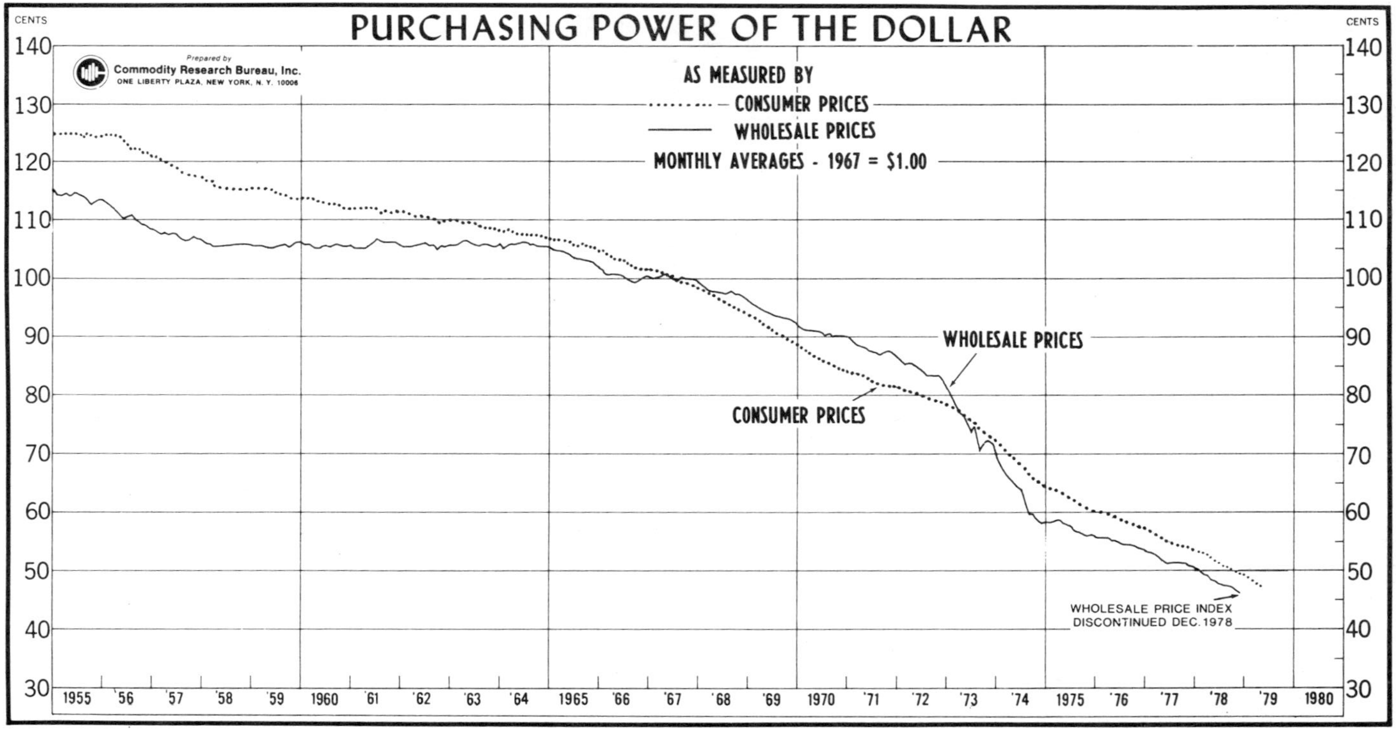

The value of your dollars sinks as prices rise. But traders in commodity futures can profit whether prices go up or down! Futures can be a hedge against both recessions and inflations.

few years later when grain set for export is embargoed by government directive. Coffee prices soared from $1.50 to $3.50 in seven months time in the wake of a crop freeze, then crashed to $2.00 as the actual extent of damage became known. Sugar rested at 10 cents for a year, then rose to 28 cents in five months as global supplies dwindled. The list of examples, as we shall see in Section Two, is almost endless.

All of us have had to deal with the effects of radical price changes, keeping abreast of big price moves and adjusting our purchases or sales accordingly. Whenever we do so, we act on principles not unlike those of the commodity futures speculator. If we go to the grocery and buy 30 pounds of sugar in the belief prices are about to skyrocket, aren't we "speculating in sugar"? If we put off buying coffee until prices drop, we're betting on the price move of a commodity. The futures exchanges offer traders an organized way of dealing with the inevitable risks of price fluctuation. On the exchanges, the trader acts much like the shopper looking for the best buy. Instead of suffering the ravages of constantly changing prices, the consumer or producer can go into the futures market and exploit the price move for his or her own financial benefit.

How does this process work? How are ordinary people like you and me able to buy and sell thousands of bushels of wheat or thousands of pork bellies (uncured bacon) or millions of dollars in government securities? We can do it because the industries that use commodities **want** us to do it, and have set up the futures exchanges to encourage us to speculate. The fact is that, without the public speculator, the futures exchange would cease to work. The futures exchange is the marketplace where the futures contracts are bought and sold, where contracts are written and where performance of the contract is guaranteed by the brokerage firms and corporations of the "clearinghouse." The economic functions of the futures markets are many and complex, and are not the subject of this book. Simply stated, the organized trade in the future purchase or sale of commodity goods provides everyone in the affected industry with a valuable cost management tool. The futures price, arrived at in the free-market of the trading floor's "pit" or "ring," represents the best consensus on the future price of a given commodity. Thus the futures price can be used as a touchstone by buyers and sellers all over the nation. It allows producers and processors to calculate, well in advance, their costs of doing business and their anticipated profit (or loss). Since the futures contract can, if so desired, be used for delivery, it serves as an alternative to the local or cash market in the commodity.

Experience and studies have shown that the futures exchanges, along with the many services they provide, would wither and die without the public speculator. Why? Because those who are in the industry that use the commodity, or that produce it, want to use the futures market to control the risk of price changes over time. They want someone else to assume that risk until the crop is harvested or the lumber purchased. Enter the speculator. The farmer who sells wheat to a speculator on the futures exchange at a good price months before a bumper crop is due **transfers the risk** of price fluctuation to the speculator. The farmer expects that, as usual, a big crop will drive prices down, which would lessen the value of the crop as compared to what it could get at present prices. The futures contract reduces the farmer's risk, for the profit on the futures contract to sell at today's high price will increase as the cash price goes down (cheap cash wheat could be delivered at the high price called for in the contract). This futures profit would largely offset the loss in value of the actual crop the farmer will harvest. The farmer in such a situation is "hedging."

On the other hand, the speculator accepts the risk in return for the right to take a profit if the price of wheat unexpectedly goes up. Maybe the speculator thinks the current crop forecast to be overly optimistic, or expects new export demand to more than compensate for the surplus supply. For a period, the speculator holds a contract to buy wheat at today's price. If in the months before harvest the price does go up, the contract for wheat can be sold on the futures exchange for a tidy profit. Meanwhile the farmer who was "hedging" will have taken a loss on the futures position, but it will be one that is largely offset by the increase in value of the anticipated crop. The constantly changing numbers and needs of producers and processors would make it impossible for them alone to establish a viable trade in futures contracts. The crowd of speculators makes it easy to buy and sell contracts. This "liquidity" of the market and its usefulness to members of the commodity's industry thus depends upon the participation of the speculator. The speculator, in turn, is lured by low margin requirements (usually 5 or 10 percent of the futures contract value) and the chance to make incredible profits. Speculators also provide the capital to run the markets, and thus to render the services in information, price analysis and brokerage that are required of an efficient trade in commodities.

What kinds of commodities can the speculator trade? Every kind, from agricultural and plant products to precious metals and financial instruments. The first futures exchanges in the United States traded mainly in the grains pouring into the market from the new farms of the mid-West. Chicago became the headquarters of futures trading, dominated by wheat and corn, while lively markets in cotton and sugar futures evolved around the export trade in New York. In the mid-1960s, successful futures contracts in live cattle, live hogs, and pork bellies transformed old ideas about what kinds of commodities could be traded. A second revolution occurred soon after when trading boomed in gold and silver futures. A third explosive innovation, following the lead of new futures contracts in foreign currencies, was the introduction of the so-called "interest rate futures," including Treasury Bills and Bonds, Government National Mortgage Association certificates (Ginnie Maes), and prime rated corporation-issued Commercial Paper. The proliferation of new contracts and the expansion of the operations of the futures exchanges themselves created unprecedented opportunities for the speculator. The speculator's advantage is that, no matter how new the contract is or how exotic the commodity, its price can only go one of three ways: up, down, or sideways. Thus all contracts can be traded with the same basic rules and methods.

The following is a list of the major exchanges and of the principal commodities traded on each:

1. **THE CHICAGO BOARD OF TRADE.** 141 W. Jackson Blvd., Chicago, IL 60604.

Iced broilers, commercial paper, corn, Ginnie Mae, gold, oats, wheat, plywood, silver, soybeans, soybean oil, soybean meal, Treasury Bonds.

2. **THE CHICAGO MERCANTILE EXCHANGE.** 444 W. Jackson Blvd., Chicago, IL 60606 (includes as a sub-division the INTERNATIONAL MONETARY MARKET)

Cattle, hogs, pork bellies, lumber, potatoes, Treasury Bills, gold, foreign currencies.

3. **COMMODITY EXCHANGE INC.** (COMEX). Four World Trade Center, New York, NY 10048.

Copper, gold, silver.

4. **MIDAMERICA COMMODITY EXCHANGE.** 175 W. Jackson Blvd., Chicago, IL 60604. (Trades "mini-contracts").

Corn, gold, hogs, oats, silver, soybeans, wheat.

5. **KANSAS CITY BOARD OF TRADE.** 4800 Main St., Kansas City, MO 64112. (Grain exchange and wheat futures market. Stock exchange contract proposed.)

Wheat.

6. **MINNEAPOLIS GRAIN EXCHANGE.** 400 South Fourth St., Minneapolis, MN 55415. (Cash market and wheat futures.)

Wheat, sunflower seeds.

7. **NEW YORK COFFEE, SUGAR, AND COCOA EXCHANGE.** Four World Trade Center, New York, NY 10048.

Coffee, sugar, cocoa.

8. **NEW YORK MERCANTILE EXCHANGE.** Four World Trade Center, New York, NY 10048.

Imported beef, platinum, potatoes, heating oil.

9. **THE NEW YORK COTTON EXCHANGE.** Four World Trade Center, New York, NY 10048.

Cotton, Frozen Orange Juice Concentrate.

10. **THE NEW YORK FUTURES EXCHANGE.** 20 Broad Street, New York, NY.

Foreign currencies, financial instruments.

Each exchange publishes a variety of **free** materials that forms a fine beginning for the speculator's trading library.

The actual mechanics of buying and selling futures contracts are relatively simple. If you wished to buy 100 shares of IBM stock, you would call your stockbroker and say "Buy 100 shares of IBM at the market price." If you wished to buy one futures contract in the pork bellies that will become your breakfast bacon, you would call your commodity broker (who may or may not also be a stockbroker) and say "Buy one May Pork Bellies at the market price." The "May" in your order signifies the **contract month** you wish to buy, as each commodity trades in month-denominated units (normally less than 12 per year). The order's details, and the price stipulated, could be varied in dozens of ways, but the procedure remains simple. Your broker will wire or phone your order to the floor of the exchange where the commodity is traded. The order will then be given to a "pit trader" who executes the actual trade.

How can this make you money? How can you profit from buying a futures contract in pork bellies? If the value of IBM stock rose after you bought, you would stand to profit. If the price of pork bellies rose after you bought, the value of the contract rises and you stand to profit. As the price of bacon in the supermarket goes up, draining dollars from other shoppers, you are making money on the deal. In other words, by buying a futures contract for pork bellies, you can actually **profit from rising prices.** In your own individual life you have "hedged" your losses in the cash world by offsetting them with futures profits:

EXAMPLE:

Stock		Futures	
Buy IBM stock at $50 per share		Buy May Pork Bellies at 40¢/lb	
Sell IBM stock at $75 per share		Sell May Pork Bellies at 47¢/lb	
Profit per share: $25		Profit per pound:	7¢
Number of shares: 100		Pounds per contract: 38,000	
Total Stock Trade Profit:	$2,500	Total Futures Trade Profit:	$2,660
Investment:	$3,750	Investment:	$1,200
Return:	67%	Return:	222%

What advantages have we gained by trading futures instead of stocks? The profits are almost equal. The differences in timing, risk, and return on invested capital, however, are dramatic. A 50 percent price move in stocks can take a very long time, possibly years. The average commodity position is held for a few days, rarely for more than a few weeks. A 7¢ move in pork bellies, with trading limits set at 4¢ per day, could take only two trading sessions. The amount of margin money required to buy the stock would be from 60-90 percent of its value. At, say, 75 percent, the stock trader would have to put up $3,750, and let it sit there for months or years waiting for a significant move in price. The margin on the pork belly contract would be about $1,200, making for a **profit of over 200 percent in two days' time.** Of course an adverse price move in bellies could wipe you out just as quickly, unless your trading method protected you against this possibility.

Who are these people trading commodities, and realizing such unheard of profits? Private and government studies profiling the "average" commodity trader reveal that he or she is much like you or me, someone with a moderate amount of capital to use as risk money and no special knowledge of the commodities traded. The boom in futures trading has brought every conceivable type of player into the futures markets. I have corresponded with traders who are bankers, farmers, ranchers, penitentiary prisoners, retired persons, secretaries, postal workers, corporation executives, doctors, blue-collar laborers and white-collar professionals. These people see futures trading as an exciting field of investment, a hedge against the increasing instability in modern economies, and as a game that challenges one's personal skills and talents.

The people who have discovered the advantages of commodity futures trading have done so despite a cloud of misconceptions that has hidden the trade and obscured its workings for many years. It's time to clear away a few of them.

The first great misconception is that it takes a great deal of money to trade commodities. The truth is exactly the opposite. Futures trading is one of the few, and one of the most practical, ways of turning a small amount of money into a fortune. Many, many traders have less than $10,000 or $15,000 invested in commodity futures. Compare this to the average stock market account of from $50,000 to $100,000. In fact, too much money invested in futures is often a handicap to successful trading. If you can't make a profit from a $5,000 account, you probably won't make a profit from a $20,000 account. Some brokers, especially those who have convinced new traders to let the brokerage firm make all the trading decisions, will require larger deposits, giving them a greater cushion for losses and more chances for commissions. A tight string on an account you manage yourself will prevent the kind of outrageous losses reported so frequently in the business. Your success at commodity trading will depend more on the skills you perfect than on the amount of money you invest. Money does not make money in commodities. The **trader** makes money, and does so by precisely planned plays that are systematically executed according to a methodical plan. Beginning with a few thousand dollars, the trader (who has presumably already practiced "on paper" for some months) can comfortably stake out positions in several markets, testing the waters. At the outset the account is traded conservatively, with an eye to sheer survival. Losses are cut strictly short, profits allowed to run, until the account grows to twice or thrice its original value. Profits should then be taken out and enjoyed, the account either closed or returned to its original state, and the process begun over again. I strongly recommend that you do not put much money into the markets until you understand completely the methods of successful trading, and have done your homework in this and other texts.

The second widely-held misconception contends that only "experts" have a chance of making profits in the dangerous game of futures trading. Common sense and the experience of hundreds of traders prove this notion false. Who is more of an "expert" about the price of potatoes, beef, pork, cooking oil, cocoa, coffee, orange juice and all the other commodities traded than today's price-conscious consumer?

Most commodity terms and names are much more familiar to us than such stock market terms as "convertible bonds," "price/earnings ratio," or "book value." Everyone understands what is meant when it is said that the price of soybeans will fall 30¢ at harvest when the bumper crop comes in. The laws of supply and demand still hold sway in most commodity markets. It may seem as if the factors determining prices are infinitely complicated and numerous, known only to the "insiders." The fact is that almost all the hard data comes from government agencies, in publications issued only on scheduled dates and prepared behind locked doors. Everyone has equal access to the information at the same time. And, at any given time, only three or four factors are changing enough to substantially influence a commodity's price. If the so-called "experts" or "insiders" at General Mills or Chase Manhattan could figure out the markets perfectly, they would do so, and the futures exchanges would be rendered useless, for there would be no uncertainty about future price changes. This hasn't happened, evidence enough to overthrow this old myth.

This is not to imply that commodity trading is a lead pipe cinch or that you can't lose money when you start trading. **You can!** The statistics are against you, as most people come out losers. The primary reason for these losses is the lack of a successful trading method and the absence of carefully developed and patiently applied trading skills. People do not lose in the markets because they have been "outfoxed" by the "experts." They have been outfoxed by themselves, or by some trading gimmick offering instant and effortless profits. If you take the time to learn well the basic approaches involved in successful trading, you will already be well ahead of most traders.

This book is designed to teach you one of these approaches, and to introduce those of you who are newcomers to the world of futures speculation. It was not designed to be a complete course in commodity trading, something you should understand from the start. What you will learn here is one simple method for buying and selling commodity futures contracts, no matter the type of commodity or the exchange involved, which exhibit a specific and identifiable price patterns. In my experience as a trader I have found this method to be the easiest, safest, and most consistently profitable system for trading commodities. **No** method is fool-proof. **No one** can guarantee you profits in the futures markets. It is for this very reason that the speculator needs a method that minimizes losses and maximizes profits. The method should also be one that is comprehensible, that can be applied by anyone of average intelligence, and which does not require dependence on a broker, advisor, or computer. The method should reduce the number of variables that go into the trading decision to the absolute minimum.

Most important, a successful trading method lets the market make the decisions. The fastest way to lose your money in the futures game is by betting against the demonstrated trend, taking positions based on the hope, fear, or rumor of a price move. The method to be taught below begins with the first law of commodity trading: The market is always right. If the market is headed in one direction, don't fight — switch. Winning commodity traders never try to outsmart the markets.

Of course there are as many systems for trading as there are traders in the markets. Commodity publications, brokerage firms and advisory service brochures advertise everything from the most sophisticated computer analysis to astrological forecasts of price cycles. Some traders "buy hogs before the holidays" or "sell wheat before the harvest."

Your order to buy or sell is executed at the commodity exchange pit or ring. Floor traders and brokers must make all trades by open public outcry, creating a genuine free market in futures contracts.

Some are disaster traders who buy and sell on the news of floods, droughts, famines, strikes, freezes or other disturbing events. Many traders wait to see what others will do, then hop aboard the bandwagon. Those who trade primarily with an eye on the factors of supply and demand are called "fundamentalists" by books on futures trading. Those who put little stock in such computations and trade instead according to the market's own price history and recent behavior are called "technicians." Most methods combine the two, but with a decided preference one way or the other.

Analysis of the fundamentals works chiefly for the forecasting of long range price moves. Fundamentals can establish the general frame of reference for particular changes in a commodity's price. But having a good idea of which direction prices should go, and why, doesn't help much if prices go the other way. Nor is it of great assistance even if the favorable move occurs, for then the trader still must evaluate the condition of the futures market and decide the best way to trade it profitably. The successful speculator cannot afford to be ignorant of the fundamentals, but the real test of skill comes in learning to trade the movements of prices as they really occur.

One key distinction ought to be kept in mind. The speculator trades prices, not physical objects. The speculator wants to buy low and sell high. It is the movement of a commodity's price that offers the potential for profits, not the commodity itself. If wheat prices sit dormant, move over to cattle or corn. Your main task is to spot the kind of movement in the price of a commodity that can return you hefty percentages of your initial outlay. The method taught in this book performs that task. The trader will learn to spot one very obvious and particular price pattern. Once spotted, that pattern gives the "signals" for when and where to buy and sell futures contracts in the commodity concerned. Many patterns have been described in the analysis of price swings. The pattern I have chosen as the foundation for the method is one that appears frequently, one that has in fact been seen in almost every commodity traded during the last ten years. It is a simple pattern to trade, one offering the trader a reasonable chance for substantial profit while exposing invested funds to a logical, moderate risk.

There are certain tools you will need to use this method of trading. Since you are trading price moves, you will need daily price quotations for the commodity futures contracts you wish to trade. Most large newspapers give a daily table of the previous day's price activity on the principal exchanges. National publications like the *Wall Street Journal* and the *New York Journal of Commerce* are excellent sources for futures prices. Or if convenient, just call or stop by your broker's office for a free, up-to-the-minute report on price activity.

If you've never read or followed futures prices before, study the sample below for a minute:

	Open	*High*	*Low*	*Settle*	*Change*	*Lifetime High*	*Lifetime Low*	*Open Interest*
CORN (CBT) — 5,000 bu; cents per bu.								
May	274½	276	272¼	275½	+ 3¼	341½	256½	44,478
July	286½	287	284½	286½	+ 2½	341	269	46,634
Sept	295½	296½	293¼	295½	+ 1½	326½	280	12,888
Dec	302	302	298½	299½	+ ½	325¼	287¼	44,375
Mar	313¼	313½	309¼	310¼	− ¼	332	299½	9,996
May	321½	322	318	318½	− 1¼	325	309	1,523

Est. vol. 46,287

This quotation would reflect the previous day's trading. The left hand column lists each of the contract months currently trading. The "May" contract opened that day at a price of 2.74½ per bushel. "High" and "Low" tell the extremes reached by the contract's price during the day's session. "Settle" gives the price at the close of trading. "Change" specifies the net difference from the close of the previous day's trade. "Lifetime High/Low" represents the highest and the lowest prices hit by the contract since the first day it began trading. "Open Interest" denotes the number of open, held contracts in the contract month as of the close of the previous day's trade. "Est. vol." represents the estimated volume of trades, both purchases and sales, in all corn contracts for the day.

The second tool for trading you will need is graph paper, on which to record and chart the changes in price. Once your system is organized and in place, it will take surprisingly little time to keep it up-dated. But be ready to commit that time, to keep up with the markets, and to watch for opportunities. If it seems bothersome or wearying at first, just calculate what your per hour salary works out to after your first winning trades!

What is the purpose of all these graphs? The trader needs a picture of the recent price action. In order to see the pattern prices are falling into, a visual display is constructed on paper that corresponds to the actual movement of prices and which dictates how best to position oneself for the future. The chart will show the market reality, the pattern of ups and downs, the trends and the ranges. On a chart you can see where prices have been, and be set to profit wherever they are going. The chart gives you a simple way to see how to position yourself in relation to price moves, where to get into a market, where to get out, when to do either and when to do neither.

Constructing a price chart is an easy procedure. On your graph paper, darken one of the vertical lines near the edge of the paper. From the base of this line, darken one of the graph paper's horizontal lines and extend it across the page. The vertical line will be your **price axis.** Each step will represent a unit change in the commodity's price. The horizontal line will be your **time axis.** Each step across will represent weeks, or months, or years.

The sample chart at the right shows fluctuations in wheat prices from June to January, at two week intervals. It is immediately apparent that this commodity's prices underwent some volatile movement, and that there were plenty of opportunities to profit for those traders who knew how to spot the patterns. Obviously the sensitivity of the chart to price changes, and the detail with which it will show price patterns, depends upon the size of the price and time increments used in its construction. Time spans greater than a month do not have enough precision; charts showing hourly price changes have too much precision. Most of the charts used in this book's illustrations record daily high, low, and settlement prices, with each darkened vertical line marking the end of another week. Remember when comparing price charts to gauge the significance of price moves; always take into account the size of both the time and price increments. The severity of a price pattern can be smoothed out or exaggerated by manipulation of these increments. If the sample price chart had been drawn with price increments of 40 instead of 20, the result would have implied a far less volatile market. To check the significance of a price pattern, calculate how much could have been lost or won by a trader holding a contract for a day, a week, or a month.

For example, take a look at the charts for the December and February Hog contracts on the following pages:

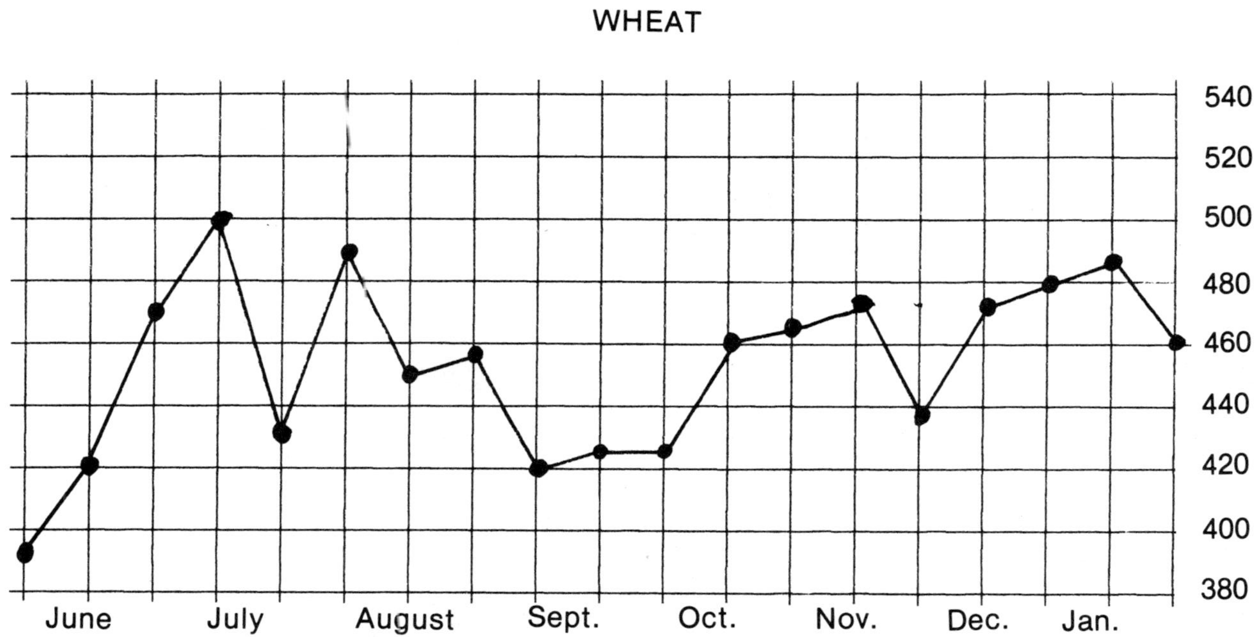

A chart provides a way to see clearly the trends and patterns of commodity futures price changes.

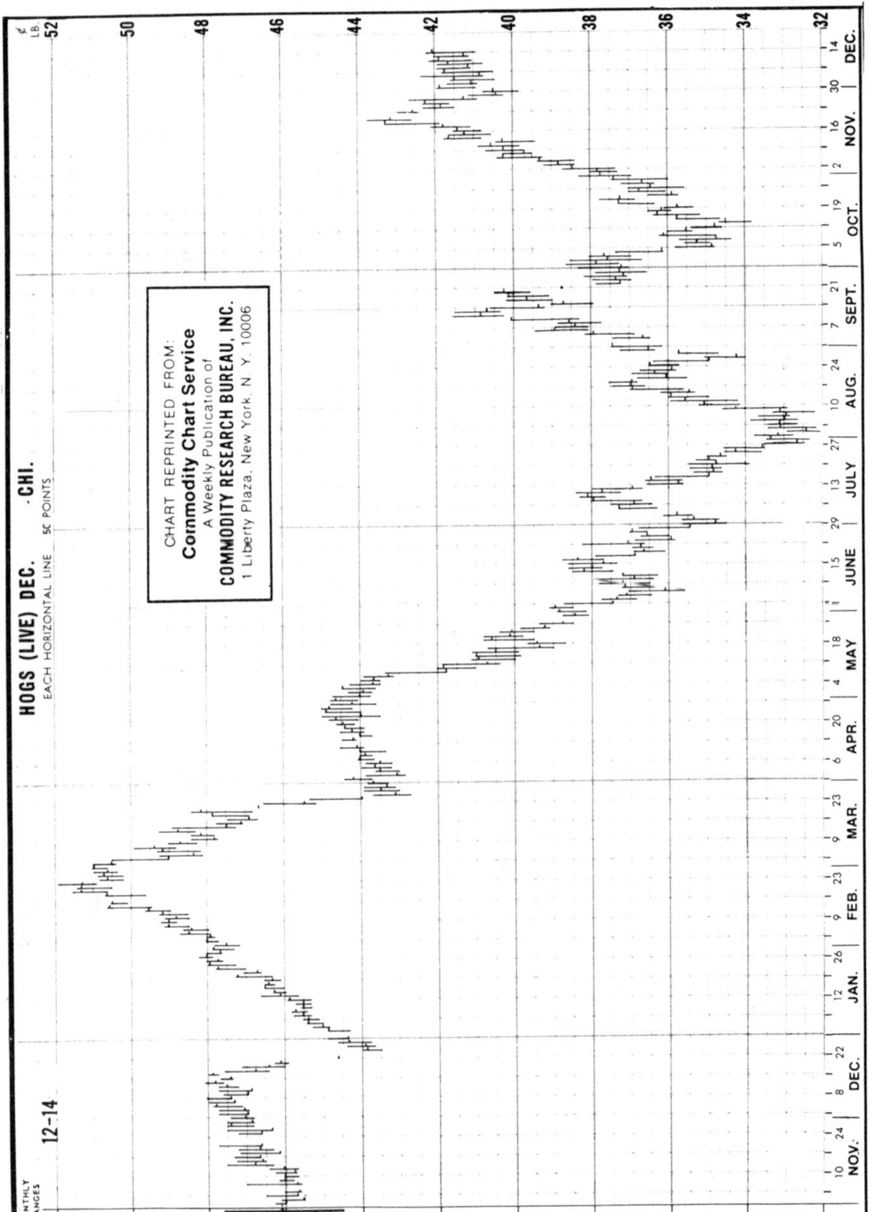
HOGS (LIVE) DEC. -CHI.
EACH HORIZONTAL LINE 50 POINTS
12-14
MONTHLY RANGES
¢ LB.
52
50
48
46
44
42
40
38
36
34
32
CHART REPRINTED FROM:
Commodity Chart Service
A Weekly Publication of
COMMODITY RESEARCH BUREAU, INC.
1 Liberty Plaza, New York, N. Y. 10006
NOV. DEC. JAN. FEB. MAR. APR. MAY JUNE JULY AUG. SEPT. OCT. NOV. DEC.

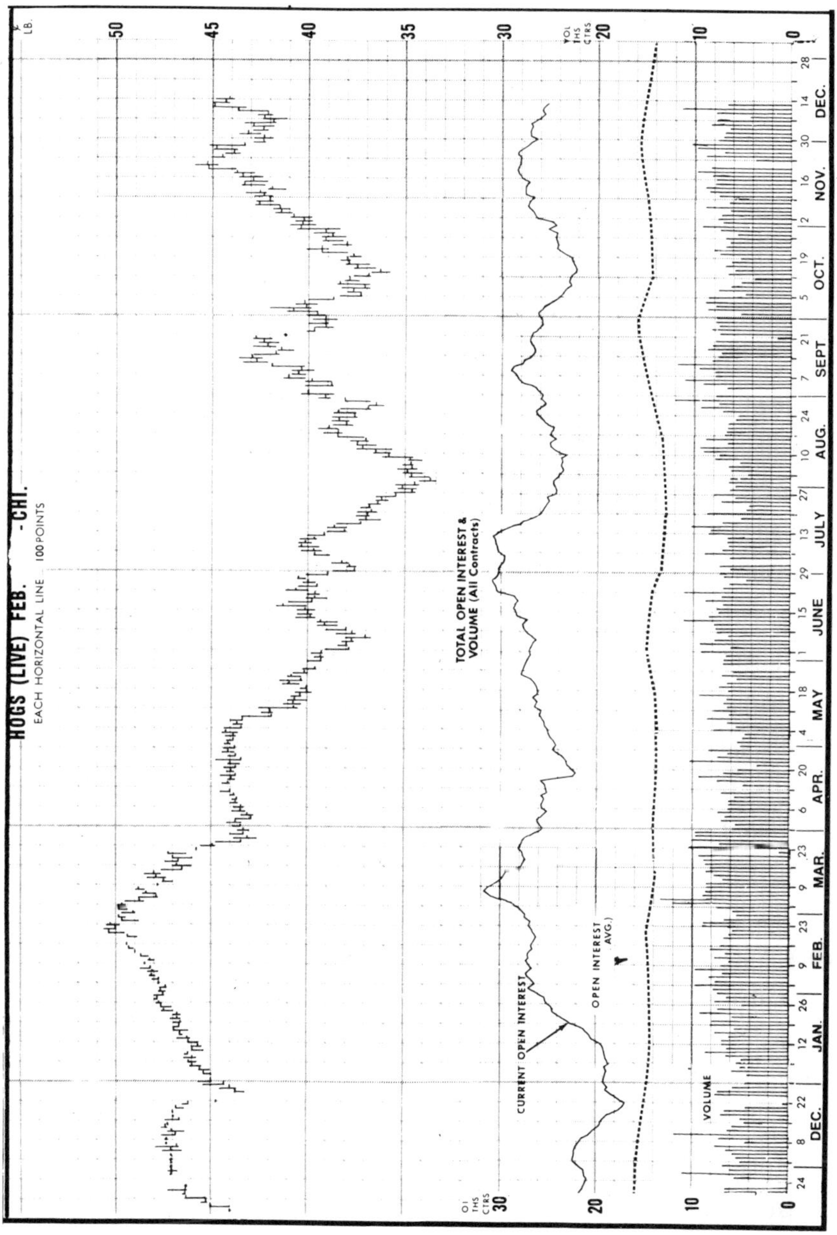

HOGS (LIVE) FEB. -CHI.
EACH HORIZONTAL LINE 100 POINTS
LB.
TOTAL OPEN INTEREST &
VOLUME (All Contracts)
CURRENT OPEN INTEREST
OPEN INTEREST AVG.)
VOLUME
OI THS CTRS
VOL THS CTRS
DEC. JAN. FEB. MAR. APR. MAY JUNE JULY AUG. SEPT OCT. NOV. DEC.

Each horizontal line on the December Live Hog contract chart represents a one-half cent per pound change in price. Extra-dark lines showing major price levels are here separated by 2 cent increments. For the February Hog contract, however, each horizontal line represents a full one cent per pound change in price, and every extra-dark line shows an increment of 5 cents per pound. The difference in the look of the charts follows accordingly, as the December chart is constructed by smaller increments and thus shows more sensitivity to price changes. At a quick glance, you might think that the price of the December contract was far more volatile than the price of the February contract. In fact, the two charts show nearly identical price moves. For example, the big price decline from February to August hits 10 extra-dark price lines on the chart for December Hogs. The decline on the chart for February Hogs (deliverable the following February) goes through only 4 extra-dark lines. Yet both contracts actually registered a similar price decline, about 17-20 cents. With every 1 cent per pound move in the price of a 30,000 pound hogs contract meaning $300 lost or won, the stakes are just as high for the February contract as for the December contract, no matter how the charts may look at first.

The best way to track the significance of price moves, and to plan exactly how to trade them, thus requires a ready knowledge of how much money is being won or lost with every "tick" or fluctuation of the commodity's price. Every time the price of wheat goes up 1 cent per bushel, for instance, simple mathematics tells us that the value of the standard 5,000 bushel contract goes up $50. Every time the price of live cattle goes down 1 cent per pound, the value of the standard 40,000 pound contract goes down $400. Similar computations can be done for each commodity traded, and the results put down in a table you should keep at hand whenever planning your trade.

FUTURES TRADING FACTS*

COMMODITY	CONTRACT SIZE	VALUE OF MOVE
British Pound	25,000 BP	$.05 = $1,250
Canadian Dollar	$100,000 CD	$.01 = $1,000
Cattle (Feeder)	42,000 Lbs	1¢ = $420
Cattle (Live)	40,000 Lbs	1¢ = $400
Cocoa	10 metric tons	$1 = $10
Coffee	37,500 Lbs	1¢ = $375
Copper	25,000 Lbs	1¢ = $250
Corn	5,000 bushels	1¢ = $50
Cotton	50,000 Lbs	1¢ = $500
Deutsche Mark	125,000 DM	1¢ = $1,250
Ginnie Mae Mtges.	$100,000 @ 8%	1% = $1,000
Gold	100 troy oz.	$1 = $100
Hogs (Live)	30,000 Lbs	1¢ = $300
Japanese Yen	12.5 Mil. JY	$.001 = $1,250
Lumber	130,000 bd. ft.	$1 = $130
Oats	5,000 bushels	1¢ = $50
Orange Juice	15,000 Lbs	1¢ = $150
Platinum	50 troy oz.	$1 = $50
Plywood	76,032 sq. ft.	$1 = $76.03
Pork Bellies	38,000 Lbs	1¢ = $380
Potatoes (NY)	50,000 Lbs	1¢ = $500
Potatoes (Chi)	80,000 Lbs	1¢ = $800
Silver	5,000 troy oz.	10¢ = $500
Soybeans	5,000 bushels	1¢ = $50
Soybean Meal	100 tons	$1 = $100
Soybean Oil	60,000 Lbs	1¢ = $600
Sugar	112,000 Lbs	1¢ = $1,120
T-Bills	$1 million	.1 = $250
T-Bonds	$100,000	1% = $1000
Wheat	5,000 bushels	1¢ = $50

* Note: *Contract specifications do change. Check with your broker for current details.*

Equipped with a knowledge of how to construct a graph, and familiar with the facts needed to interpret the chart's meaning, the speculator can read the price action of any commodity. The visual display of the chart reveals the fluctuations, sometimes mild and sometimes extreme, of commodity prices as they respond to changes in supply and demand. No one needs to be a university scholar to know that with abundance comes low prices, and with scarcity comes high prices. How does a period of abundant supply appear on a commodity futures price graph?

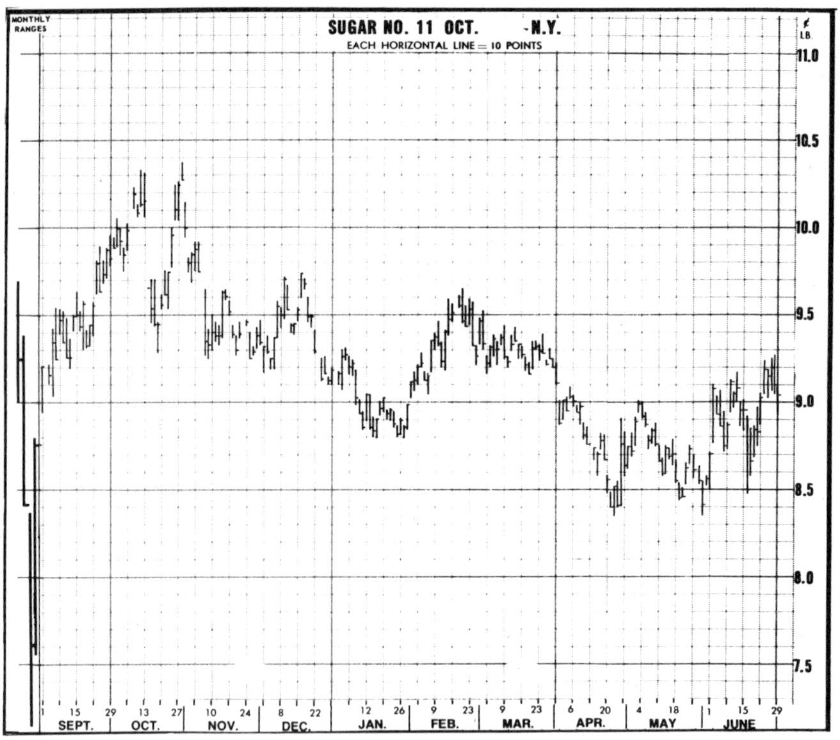

Sugar, as every grocery shopper knows, has been a volatile commodity during the last decade. It is a "world" crop, subject to the uncertainties of weather and production in numerous producing nations around the globe. The October Sugar chart presents a close up view of sugar futures prices during a period of relative calm. The price line appears to have many sharp ups and downs, but these are partly explained by the sensitivity of the chart, which shows major increments at every one-half cent level. The price of sugar futures fluctuated in a **range of only 2 cents** during these ten months. Certainly there were some profit opportunities, but none were very large or very sustained. Ample supplies dampened the volatility of sugar prices. Not for long, however.

Examine now the chart for May Sugar:

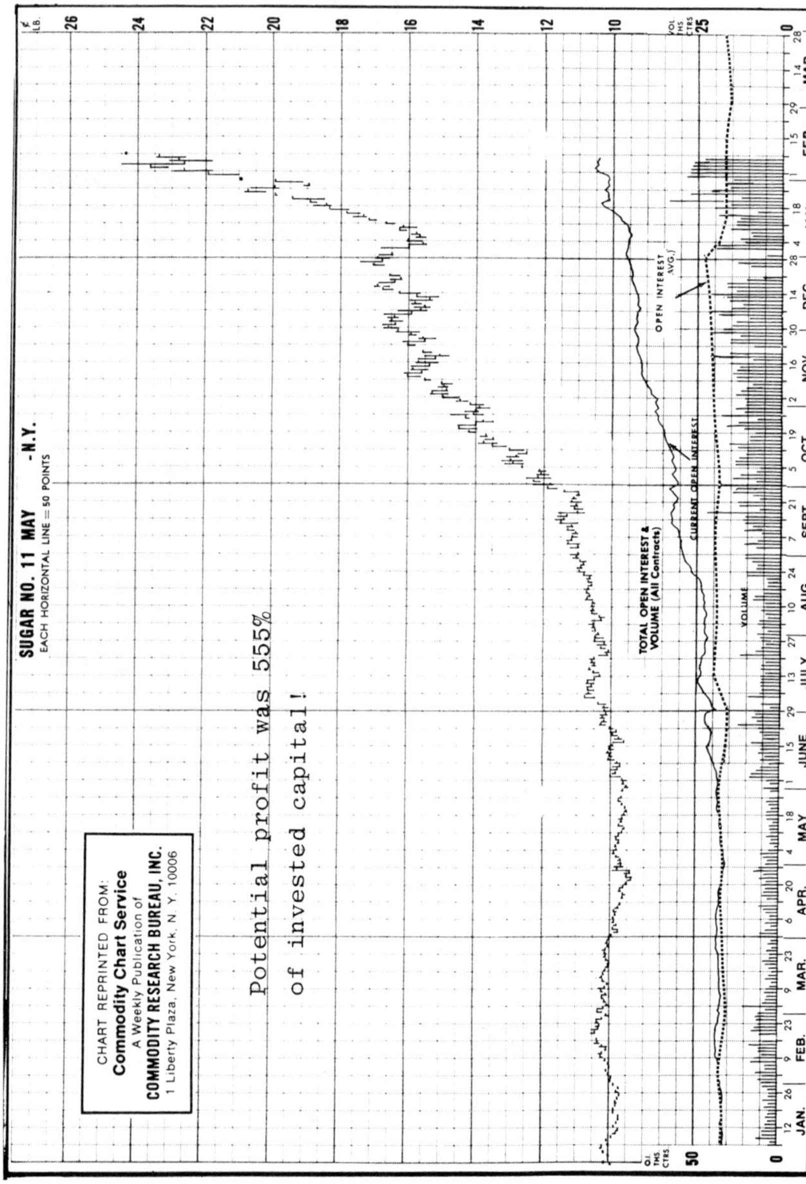
SUGAR NO. 11 MAY -N.Y.
EACH HORIZONTAL LINE = 50 POINTS
CHART REPRINTED FROM:
Commodity Chart Service
A Weekly Publication of
COMMODITY RESEARCH BUREAU, INC.
1 Liberty Plaza, New York, N. Y. 10006
Potential profit was 555%
of invested capital!
TOTAL OPEN INTEREST & VOLUME (All Contracts)
CURRENT OPEN INTEREST
OPEN INTEREST AVG.)
VOLUME
JAN. FEB. MAR. APR. MAY JUNE JULY AUG. SEPT. OCT. NOV. DEC. JAN. FEB. MAR.

The left hand side represents the same action portrayed in the previous sugar chart. The price line has been considerably smoothed out by the use of 2 cent incremental units rather than one-half cent levels. This better represents the quiet nature of the sugar market during the first half of the year, and makes it possible to chart the dramatic price rise that occurred in the following months. Sugar prices took off, more than **doubling in six months' time.** The former estimates of sugar supplies and coming harvests had been tossed aside as new information suggested a world-wide shortage. The reports from Cuba were of an almost total failure of the year's sugar crops. So the futures markets in sugar took off with news of scarcity. Unless a corrective crash intervened, the message was for eventually higher prices at the grocery store.

Cereals, ice cream, candy, processed foods of every kind, soda pop, lemonade, dozens of our supermarket staples contain sugar. The price of each and every one must rise with the rise in sugar prices, and more dollars be taken out of the pockets of unprotected consumers. The same laws of abundance, scarcity, and ripple-effect price rises holds for all the other commodities, even money itself. When the U.S. Federal Reserve Board decides to "tighten credit," it reduces the supply of dollars available to the nation's businesses and consumers. The scarcity of money means that the price of money — interest rates — goes up. The "interest rate" futures markets came into being as a way to reduce the risks of such fluctuations in the price of money, and they operate according to the same basic principles as the markets in wheat, soybeans, or cattle.

Look back now at the chart for May Sugar. It also illustrates how investors who chose to use the futures markets could profit from rising prices, making very large sums on a modest amount of risk capital. One single futures contract in sugar contains 112,000 pounds. If you buy one May Sugar futures contract, you are buying the right to 112,000 pounds of sugar, delivered in May at the price you now pay. A speculator in the May Sugar futures contract could have bought at a price of 12 cents per pound in October. (As we shall soon learn, the choice of this particular time and price was a result of method, not accident.) The margin requirement for one sugar contract was then $2,000. A mere $2,000 controlled the right to profit (or be ruined) by the change in value of 112,000 pounds of sugar.

What happened? The chart tells the happy story. May Sugar hit a high of 24.5 cents, then dropped back to 22 cents. Let us say that our trader figures that, at this point, sugar has crested and it's time to take the money and run. The profit per pound is 10 cents. Our "Trading Facts" let us quickly calculate the total **profit on a single contract at $11,200.** This translates into a return of over **500 percent** on invested capital in only four months. A detailed breakdown would look like this:

COMMODITY: Sugar
EXCHANGE: N.Y. Coffee, Cocoa, & Sugar
MARGIN REQUIRED: $2,000
PURCHASE PRICE (October): 12¢ per/lb
SALES PRICE (February): 22¢ per/lb

PROFIT PER/POUND:	10¢
POUNDS PER/CONTRACT	112,000
GROSS PROFIT:	$11,200
BROKERAGE FEE:	$75
NET PROFIT:	$11,125
CAPITAL INVESTED:	$2,000
RETURN ON CAPITAL:	555%
TIME PERIOD:	4 Months

As this text proceeds, the reader will find, through inspection of actual market case histories, that the profits on this sugar trade are neither abnormal nor unique. Such opportunities happen literally every year, and in a number of different commodities. The possible returns on some may dwarf those of the above example. Consider for a moment the case of September Cocoa:

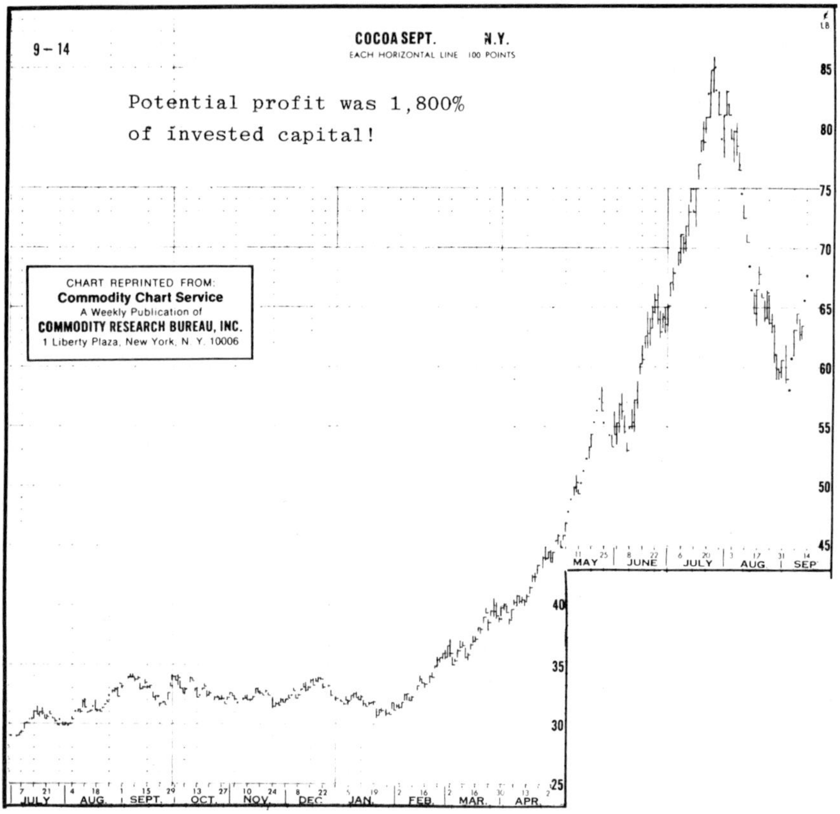
9 – 14
COCOA SEPT. N.Y.
EACH HORIZONTAL LINE 100 POINTS
Potential profit was 1,800%
of invested capital!
CHART REPRINTED FROM:
Commodity Chart Service
A Weekly Publication of
COMMODITY RESEARCH BUREAU, INC.
1 Liberty Plaza, New York, N. Y. 10006
¢ LB
85
80
75
70
65
60
55
50
45
40
35
30
25
JULY
AUG.
SEPT.
OCT.
NOV.
DEC.
JAN.
FEB.
MAR.
APR.
MAY
JUNE
JULY
AUG
SEP

The price of cocoa creeps along for 8 months between 30 and 35 cents, then zooms upwards to a high of 85 cents in only 4 months time. The cause was a scarcity of cocoa, registered in the above chart and eventually in the grocery store.

A breakdown of a trade in September Cocoa futures most anyone could have made would have looked something like this:

COMMODITY: Cocoa
CONTRACT SIZE: 30,000 lbs (old contract size)
MARGIN REQUIRED: $750

PURCHASE PRICE:	35¢ per/lb
SALES PRICE:	80¢ per/lb
PROFIT PER/POUND:	45¢
POUNDS PER CONTRACT:	30,000
GROSS PROFIT:	$13,500
BROKERAGE FEE:	$60
NET PROFIT:	$13,440
RETURN ON CAPITAL:	1,792%
TIME PERIOD:	5 Months

Before going on to more examples, and to the mechanics of the trading method, a review of four basic principles underlying futures trading will be of help. The case histories of sugar and cocoa were based, we can see in retrospect, on one of these principles:

> PRINCIPLE #1: In commodities, wherever the cash price of a commodity goes, the futures price of that same commodity will generally follow.

The utility of the futures markets absolutely depends upon this close relationship of cash and futures prices. History shows, time and again, that futures contracts and futures markets that are not in a close correspondence with the commodity's cash markets will inevitably fail. Futures prices are not pure speculation subject to the mere whims and emotions of traders. They are framed and bound by the actual cash prices paid for goods in the real world. Futures prices may fluctuate in a range a bit above or below cash prices, but never very far. If they did, traders would buy futures and deliver against cash, or vice versa, effectively checking the imbalance. In practice, as the charts to the right show, the harmony is consistent.

A careful inspection of the charts reveals a further significant fact supporting the principle. Notice that, from May through December, the prices shown on the May Pork Bellies futures chart are continually higher than those shown on the Cash Pork Bellies chart. The **price patterns** remain almost identical, but a price differential separates them. That differential grows smaller, and almost disappears, after January. In October the difference was about 10 cents; by mid-April it is only 5 cents. During those "distant" months, the futures price was "guessing" where cash would be many months later. As the May contract approaches the month of May, when the futures contracts can be delivered, the time differential has shrunk from months to weeks. Soon the futures contracts, unless liquidated by those holding them, will turn into vehicles for the delivery of cash products.

Here is the reason why futures prices and cash prices generally follow each other so closely. The contracts for future delivery can be and sometimes are used for actual commodity transactions, thus binding their prices to the going prices on the regular cash markets. The futures

PORK BELLIES (FROZEN) MAY · CHI.
EACH HORIZONTAL LINE = 100 POINTS
¢ LB
55
50
45
40
35
30
25
1 15 29 13 27 10 24 7 21 5 19 2 16 30 14 28 4 18 1 15 29 14 28 11 25 9
JUNE JULY AUG. SEPT. OCT. NOV. DEC. JAN. FEB. MAR. APR MAY

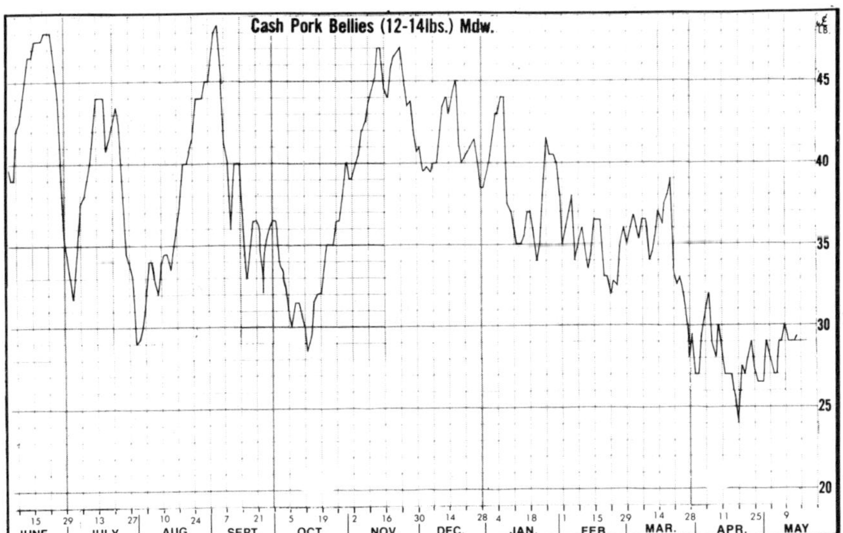
Cash Pork Bellies (12-14lbs.) Mdw.
¢ LB.
45
40
35
30
25
20
15 29 13 27 10 24 7 21 5 19 2 16 30 14 28 4 18 1 15 29 14 28 11 25 9
JUNE JULY AUG. SEPT. OCT. NOV. DEC. JAN. FEB. MAR. APR. MAY

exchanges spend thousands of hours and dollars in writing these standard contracts, consulting with potential industry users in order to come up with contracts that are both useful for speculative purposes and practical for cash business. Remember, the commodity trader does not literally buy and sell "commodities." Rather, the trader buys and sells pieces of paper known as "futures contracts."

A futures contract is a legal document which calls for the delivery of an actual commodity at some prescribed time in the future. As the cash price of the commodity fluctuates, so will the value of that piece of paper. Prices can make large moves up and down many months before the delivery date, providing speculators with the chance to get in and out of the markets (hopefully for a profit) long before the contract falls due for delivery. If you hold the right to receive delivery of 5,000 bushels of corn, the value of your paper futures contract will generally move in the direction of cash prices. If the cash price goes up and the futures price follows, you profit. If the cash price goes down and futures follow, you lose. On the other hand, if you hold the right to deliver corn, the value of your paper futures contract will generally move in the **opposite** direction of cash prices. If the cash price goes down, you can "buy back" your promise to sell, and profit. If the price goes up, you will have to "buy back" at a higher price than you sold at, and you lose. Whether you are trading in silver or soybeans, the value of your piece of paper generally follows the price paid for that commodity at the cash marketplace, be it Switzerland or Chicago.

Therefore, as a trader in commodity contracts, you will want to **buy** futures contracts if you expect a **rise** in the actual commodity's price, and **sell** futures contracts if you anticipate a **decline** in the price of the cash commodity. If the evidence suggests hog prices have begun an upward swing that should last for 10 or 20 cents, the speculator will consider seriously **buying** hog futures contracts. If a housing boom collapses and lumber prices start down, the trader will look hard at the possibility of **selling** lumber or plywood futures contracts.

The second principle that concerns us, and that serves as the key to the method for making a fortune in commodities, also relates to cash commodity prices:

> PRINCIPLE #2: When cash prices advance or decline out of a long narrow trading range, they usually continue to advance or decline for several weeks or months before returning to their original price level.

Think about this principle a moment, if you will. Imagine its application to the price of milk at the grocery store. Ample supplies have kept prices steady at 50 cents a quart for many months. One day you go to the dairy case and discover that milk has risen in price to 52 cents. What has caused this rise in price after so long a period of stability?

The law of supply and demand has exercised it's power. The supply of milk available at 50 cents a quart has simply been exhausted. With the demand for milk not satisfied, the price had to rise. Whether demand pushed the price up, or a scarcity of actual milk, the old, longstanding price equation has been shattered. Once the price of milk has moved out of it's former range, it will continue upward in it's new direction as far and as fast as the market will allow. Whatever reason drove milk prices to abandon their old levels and seek higher ground will continue to exercise its influence until its strength is exhausted. If that reason, or combination of reasons, had the power to break through a price level that had held good for months, chances are it has the power to cause prices to move in the new direction for an appreciable period of time. Once prices have hit 52 cents, it would be reasonable

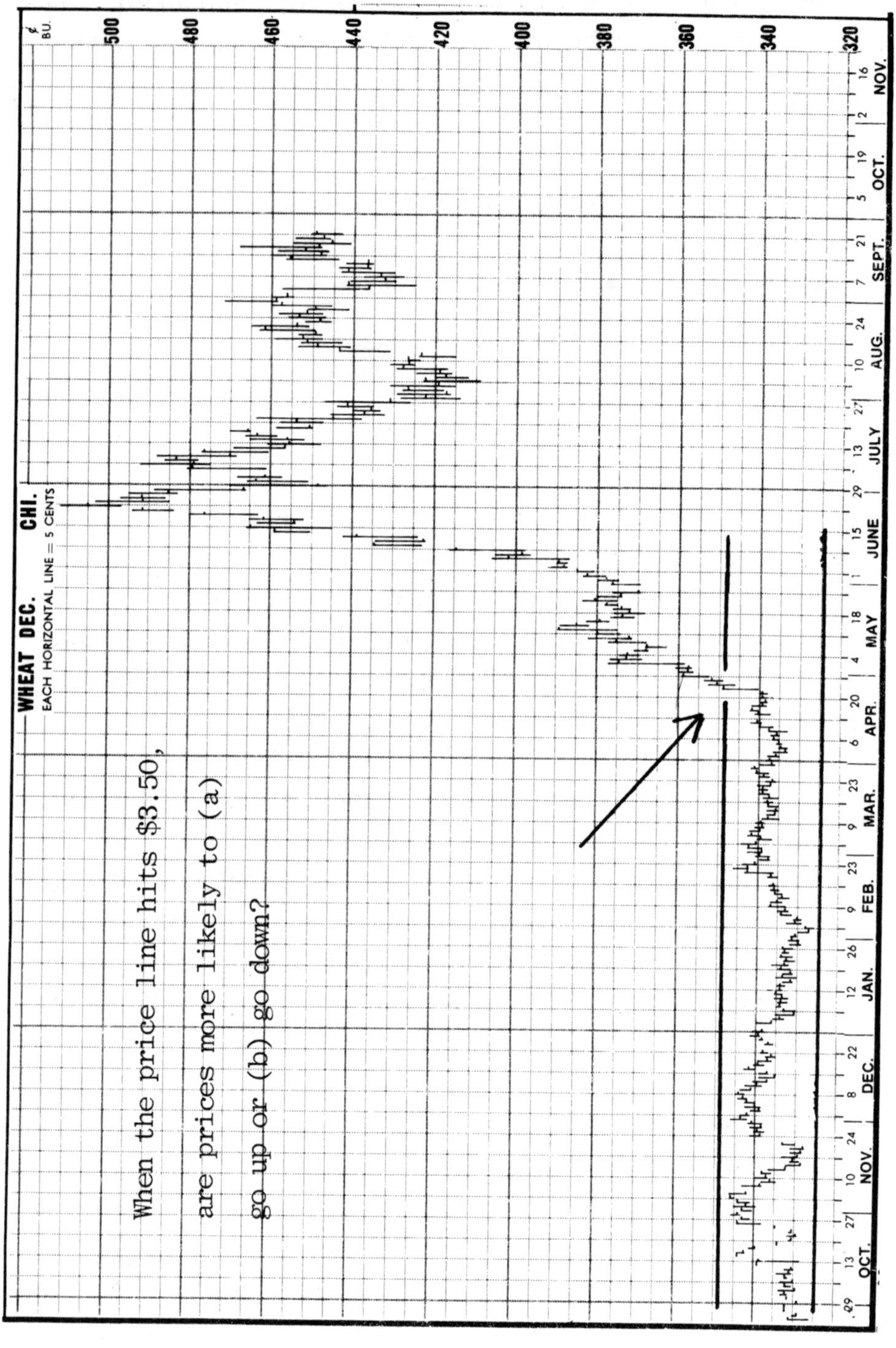
WHEAT DEC. CHI.
EACH HORIZONTAL LINE = 5 CENTS
¢ BU.
500
480
460
440
420
400
380
360
340
320
OCT. NOV. DEC. JAN. FEB. MAR. APR. MAY JUNE JULY AUG. SEPT. OCT. NOV.
When the price line hits $3.50,
are prices more likely to (a)
go up or (b) go down?

to expect them to reach 53, 54, 55, and so on before (if ever) they fall back to 50 cents.

Here we are not concerned with minor price fluctuations, or markets that have been swinging up and down continuously for weeks or months. A successful trading method selects the markets it will trade very carefully, isolating the ones that exhibit characteristics that promise the best chances for a profitable trade. The trader who knows the business doesn't worry about sitting out for days or even weeks. Patiently, the speculator keeps the charts and watches the prices, waiting for a price pattern to form that can easily, and with minimal risk, be exploited for hefty returns. In our case, we're watching for markets that have shown very little fluctuation in prices over considerable periods of time, usually weeks or months. We are preparing ourselves for the moment when prices shatter the old sideways pattern and move dramatically upward or downward. It doesn't matter why. What matters is that the old trend be long enough, and the new price move big enough, to qualify for trading by our method.

Now let's do a case study. On the wheat chart you have a period of relatively stable prices followed by a sharp price advance out of the previously narrow trading range (called by some chart makers a "channel"). When prices moved through the $3.50 mark, what should experienced traders have expected? For six months the price of wheat had hovered between $3.25 and $3.45. Suddenly, at the beginning of May, prices continue to climb past the $3.45 ceiling of the previous trading range, hitting $3.75 by May 2. At $3.50, five cents above the highest point reached by the December contract in six months, was the price more likely to (a) go up or (b) go down? Common sense and Principle #2 answer (a), up.

In just two months time, the December contract hit $5.10 before suffering a corrective drop into the $4.20-$4.60 range. What drove wheat prices up? Most likely it was a radical change in the fundamental supply and demand statistics for the commodity. The wheat harvest in the United States usually begins in early summer. Clearly, throughout the winter, wheat from the old crop had been in ample supply, keeping prices steady. In late April, the old crop appeared to traders too small to adequately cover demand until the new crop could reach the market. The squeeze was on. Prices on the cash and futures markets both soared as the scarcity of wheat drove prices sky-high. Once new crop wheat began to reach the cash markets in July, the scarcity eased and prices dropped, though they remained above the old levels, perhaps in an effort to "ration" the wheat supply over the coming year.

But the speculator following Principle #2 didn't have to know any of this (though it would have helped confirm the signals). Whatever the reason for the price move, the observation that one must make is that after a period of relative stability, once prices move out of that narrow range they normally tend to continue to move in that direction for several days, weeks, or months. This is an **essential market observation** which will be of the utmost importance to you as a commodity futures trader. While it may seem too simple, you should remember that something need not be complex for you to make money from it. A great many people have lost their shirts in the commodity markets precisely because their approach or analysis was too complicated.

It is impossible to forecast all commodity price fluctuations, or even the majority of them. So, rather than attempt to trade all the markets all the time, some speculators limit trading to a particular price pattern that has shown itself consistently to be profitable. My experience in 15 years of commodity futures trading has convinced me that the "breakout from a narrow range" pattern offers more profits, more often, and with less risk than any other. It is a pattern that returns, because of the ongoing force of the breakout, substantial profits to those who wait patiently and then climb aboard. The speculator in December Wheat who bought at $3.50 and sold at $5.00 would have made $7,500 (minus commissions) in just two months, a profit of **500 percent** on the required margin of $1,500.

Waiting for a commodity's price to actually make its move out of the old sideways channel eliminates much of the danger one can run into when playing the markets by a price forecasting method. The uncertainties of price forecasting, and of trading on the basis of such forecasts, have been exhibited countless times (to the ruin of many speculators). In 1963, it was rumored in financial circles that the United States government would stop selling silver from its treasury stocks. Economists forecast that, when the government sales halted, the demand for silver would be so great and the supply so small that the price of silver would jump from its 1963 average of $1.25 per troy ounce to above $2.00. Commodity futures traders who understood Principle #1 knew that when the cash price of silver rose, the value of silver futures contracts would also rise. So, in 1963, traders throughout the world bought futures contracts for silver. **Expecting** a substantial price rise, they bought and they bought and they bought.

But the United States government didn't stop selling silver from its stocks in 1963, and the price didn't rise to $2.00 an ounce. It rose a little, to $1.29, and then sat there. In 1964, rumors once more forecast a cutoff of government silver supplies, exciting more traders to buy silver. The rumors were just that — rumors. The forecasts were wrong, and silver closed the year where it began, at $1.29. The same story repeated itself in 1965 and 1966. The traders who had bought silver futures watched their money sit dormant, or took small profits and losses while waiting for the big move.

The successful speculator, however, stood apart from this crowd. This trader also knew that the cash price of silver would take the futures price with it, and believed that a halt in government sales would drive silver prices up substantially. But, unlike the thousands of other silver traders, this speculator knew better than to bet money on a **belief.** Charts and careful planning were substituted for forecasts, rumors, and hopes. When and if silver prices rose to $2.00, they would have to pass through $1.35 to get there. Silver futures hadn't broken that level for years, so it was reasonable to assume that a move through this barrier signalled a strong uptrend. So, rather than just hoping for a price advance in silver, the trader decided to buy futures contracts **only if** prices actually did rise. This trader, being a wise investor and methodical speculator, called the brokerage house and gave one simple order:

> "Buy 10 silver contracts for me at $1.35 an ounce
> Stop/GTC."

This kind of order is called a "stop order." It instructs the broker to buy 10 silver futures contracts for the trader **if,** and only if, the price rises to $1.35. If the price does hit $1.35, the "floor broker" or "pit trader" at the exchange who is charged with executing the speculator's order will now treat it as a "market order," filling it at the best price available. But if the price never rises to $1.35, then no trade is executed and no contracts purchased. A "stop order" is activated only if the specified price is hit. The trader could have placed this order in 1963 and just let it sit, "GTC," good-till-cancelled. No

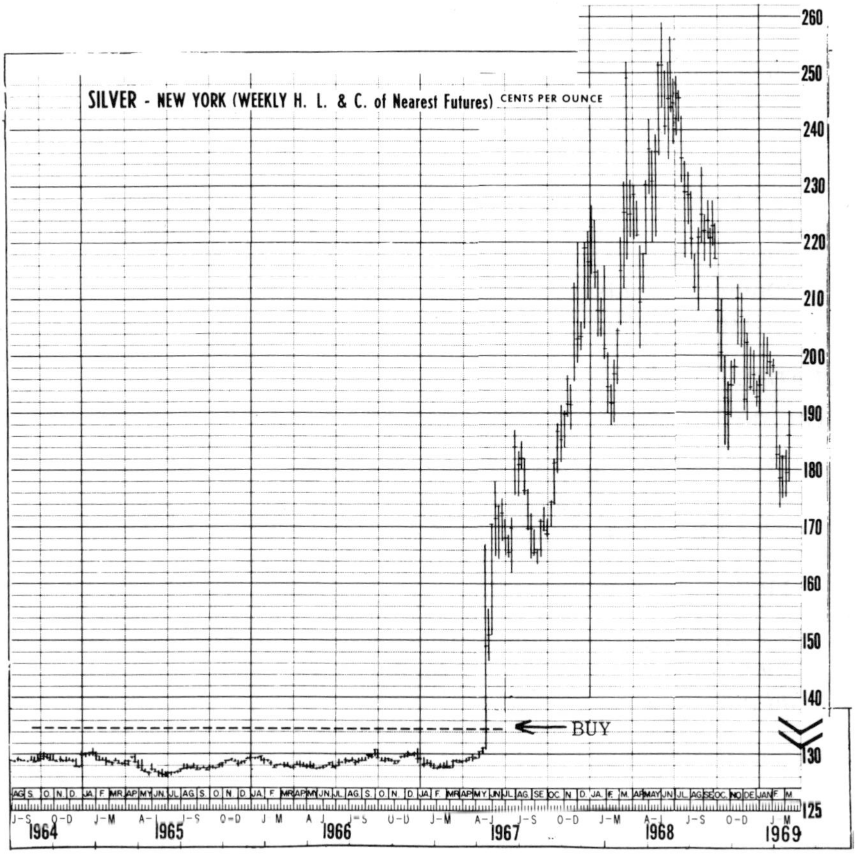

Don't bet on rumors, fears or hopes. Make your trades only when the market actually starts to move.

commission is charged unless the order is actually executed. For four years the order sat. The trader kept out of a profitless market, yet was stationed for quick entry when the move came. No risk capital was tied up in mere hopes.

This trader could withstand the pressure of rumors, professional advice or broker's recommendations because of strict adherence to the principles of successful futures trading:

> PRINCIPLE #3: Since futures prices follow cash prices, **never** buy commodity futures contracts **unless** you anticipate an advance in cash prices. **Never** sell commodity futures contracts **unless** you anticipate a decline in cash prices.

Yet Principle #3 won't be of any help at all, as the case of the silver market shows, without a further rule:

> PRINCIPLE #4: If you do decide to buy, **don't buy until** prices actually do advance. If you do decide to sell, **don't sell until** prices actually do decline.

Mark Twain once wrote:

> *A cat, having sat upon a hot stove lid, will not sit upon such again. . . . but then neither will he sit on a cold stove lid either.*

By 1967 many silver traders were like Twain's cat. They had been burned by an inactive market. Tired of wasting their money and discouraged about the possibility of the big move in silver, most had left the market and turned to corn, or cotton, or soybeans. The wise speculator, however, at no cost in money or patience, kept renewing the "stop order." Finally, on May 18, 1967, the Treasury Department suddenly called a press conference in Washington to make a hurried announcement:

> *Gentlemen and ladies, we wish to advise the press and financial community that as of 5:00 p.m. today, the United States Treasury will cease all sales of silver except to domestic users.*

That was all the spokesperson said, but it was enough, as a look back at the silver futures chart reveals. The price of silver in both the cash and futures markets ascended dramatically. As it pushed through the $1.35 level, the "stop order" of our trader was "tripped," and the 10 contracts purchased (the actual price paid will vary, up or down, according to conditions in the trading pit itself). Then the successful trader watched gleefully as the price continued climbing past $2.00 until it peaked at $2.60.

Then, as is inevitable with any price move, the reversal set in. Since prices were now well above the trader's $2.00 goal, and since previous reversals showed some weakness in this bull market, the trader decided to liquidate. Since prices were actually going down, it was time to sell. When price hit $2.30, the speculator called the broker and said "Sell 10 silver contracts 'at the market.' " This order would be executed immediately by the floor trader at the best price available in the market.

Let us say that the contracts were purchased at $1.35, and sold at $2.25. At that time and for that silver contract (different from today's), the required capital investment would have been $9,000. The realized profit on the total ten contracts would have been $135,000 — a return of 1,500% in less than 8 months time. How long would it take to make such a return if the money had been placed in a passbook savings account? About 200 years!

What you have just seen is a glimpe into one method for trading in the commodity futures markets. (I have written about others in my more detailed *Manual*.) Don't be fooled by the fact that the silver trade I have described took place in the 1960s. The year or the type of commodity doesn't matter. The principles hold true, and are all the more impressive for having worked, year in and year out, on countless markets.

Each year commodity prices fluctuate between highs and lows. Often the profit can be as unbelievably large as you have just seen. Large returns are not offered every year in every commodity. But large price moves in the pattern we have isolated do occur each year in some particular commodity, on some commodity exchange, at some time. That is one reason why the trader will want to keep an eye, and a chart, on several markets, while waiting for a profitable trading opportunity to reveal itself. What is required are four basic skills:

1. Learn to identify price patterns where price has remained in a narrow trading range for a significant period of time, and then advanced or declined markedly out of that narrow channel.
2. Learn when to buy, and when to sell, in response to such market moves. Learn to use "stop-orders."
3. Learn the technique for protecting your futures position and conserving your profits. As we shall soon see, the skillful use of "stop-loss" orders will generally enable you to get out of the market with a manageable loss should the market price move adversely in relation to your position.
4. Learn the technique for letting your profits run, maximizing returns should your futures positions be on the right side of a price move.

These skills apply to every commodity and every commodity futures contract traded on every commodity futures exchange. Whether you are trading in wheat, soybeans, silver, plywood, Treasury Bills or heating oil, their application will be the same. Learn these skills and you have a very good chance of making considerable profits from your commodity trading. In the second half of this book, we will discuss these skills in detail, and apply them to actual markets.

SECTION TWO

THE METHOD AND THE MARKETS

II

Commodity futures is a high-speed, high-risk, high-reward marketplace. New contract months begin trading as soon as the old expire. New individual contracts come and go, sometimes in seconds, as traders establish or liquidate positions. If you miss a price move in a commodity, don't worry. There will always be another chance soon, in one commodity or another. As long as prices fluctuate, there will be traders willing to buy and sell for a profit. The successful trader plans to go where prices go, when they go, keeping the trading ship afloat and sailing even as the winds and waves toss all around. A profitable voyage comes from the skillful exploitation of forces which, if one were to resist them or play them wrong, can quickly sink the most expensively outfitted investment vehicle.

We left you at the end of the first section of this book with a list of four basic skills required of successful futures traders. These skills, it was asserted, are equally applicable no matter what the commodity traded — wheat, soybean oil, T-Bonds or silver. The substance doesn't affect the method. Why? Because prices for a product can only go one of three ways: up, down, or sideways. There are no other choices. The method you are now learning is designed to profit from a commodity which **first** goes sideways for a significant period of time **and then** advances **or** declines out of that sideways price trend. It is as simple as that.

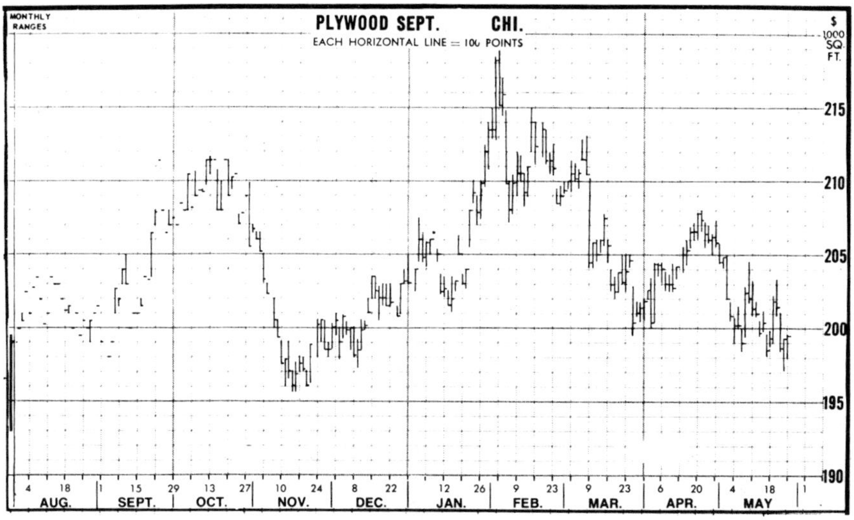

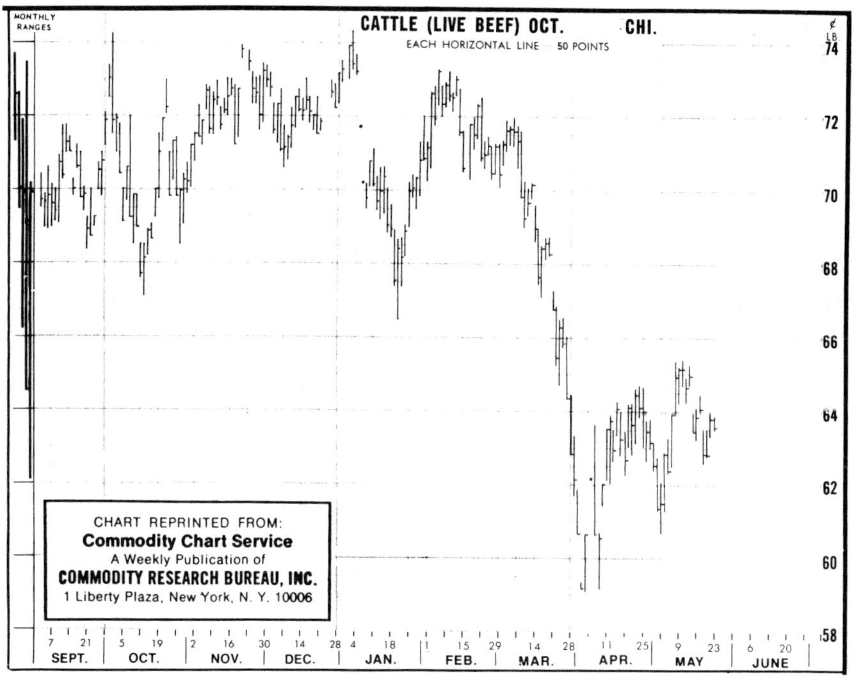

Do these volatile markets qualify for method trading?

We found that three steps were necessary elements in the method of our trading program. First, collection of commodity futures prices on a regular and steady basis. Second, accurate and up-to-date recording of prices for commodities the speculator is interested in trading. Third, transfer of daily price quotations from these records to a piece of graph paper in order to better visualize price histories and trends. Such charts enable the trader to determine, at a glance, the direction of prices — up, down, or sideways. (Professional charts, such as all those used in this text, may be purchased from a number of subscription chart services.) Learn to use these tools, through practice and patience, and you'll be on your way to creating your own independent system for successful trading.

Where do you start with your newly acquired tools? First, learn to spot the kind of market that qualifies for trading according to the method. Not every market qualifies. The trader should be able to recognize profitable markets with a short glance at the charts. On the preceding and following pages are some typical commodity futures price graphs of the type we have been discussing. You could have maintained such graphs on your own using daily prices out of the newspaper, or received them through subscription to a service. Either way, the charts tell you where the market has been, where it stands, and where it is likely to be headed. Examine the charts for September Plywood and October Live Cattle. Do these contracts, according to the charts, qualify for trading with the method we have been learning? Are prices in these graphs fluctuating in a narrow range over a long period of time? Clearly they are not. Fluctuation in a narrow price range should be the first characteristic the speculator checks for on the chart.

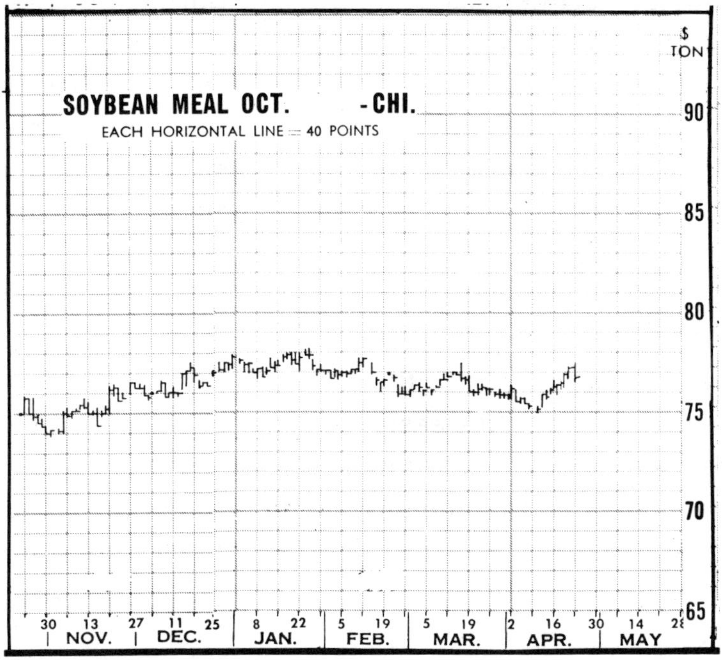

Are these contracts candidates for method trading?

Now look at the charts for October Soybean Meal and July Platinum. Do they qualify? Yes, they are strong potential candidates for trading by our method. Soybean meal has been fluctuating in a range of about $3 a ton for five months (or only about $300 per contract). Platinum hasn't moved much beyond a range of $8 per ounce for 6 months (or only about $400 per contract). No one would want to hold a position in these markets, as they are not offering any substantial profits. But they do signal the methodical trader to watch for the breakout. The longer the time period in which prices trade within a narrow range, the easier that market will generally be to trade for the commodity futures speculator.

The moment of truth comes when the trader tries to spot the actual breakout. For the method to work, price must eventually move out of an established trading range by a meaningful advance or decline:

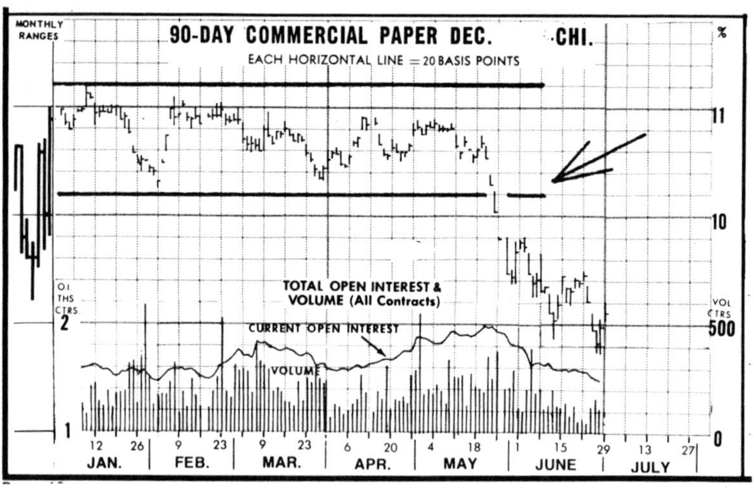

DECLINE OUT OF TRADING RANGE

ADVANCE OUT OF TRADING RANGE

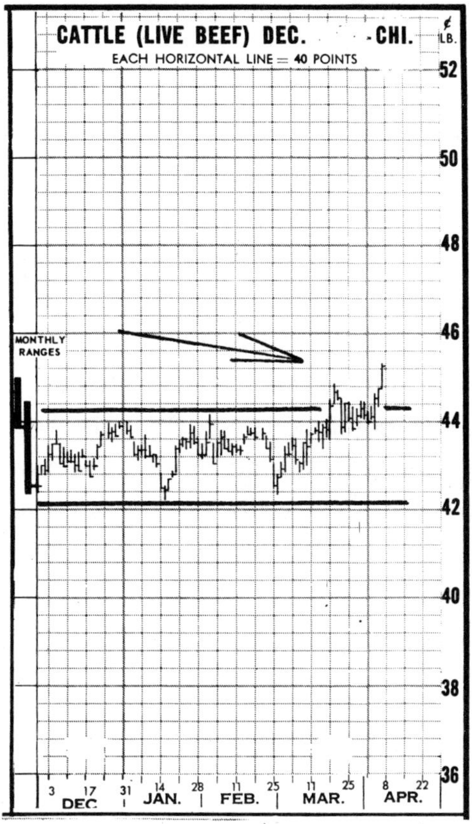

The charts for December Cattle and December Commercial Paper indicate price movements departing from clearly defined channels. These contracts would become serious contenders for trading, as they have demonstrated both a long-standing sideways trend and a sharp move above or below that trend. The trader in cattle will consider buying futures contracts (going "long"). The trader in commercial paper will consider selling futures contracts (going "short").

What causes formerly quiet commodities to suddenly rise or fall in price? Most often, the weeks or months (or even years) of sideways price patterns imply a balanced and unchanging supply and demand situation. If something occurs to radically upset that balance, altering the fundamentals for the commodity, the breakout will probably follow. Thus another indicator for the method trader will be a relatively stable supply and demand relationship for the commodity over a substantial period of time. Look back for a moment to the silver chart and its price surge. Notice how once demand for silver achieved dominance over available supply, this economic situation was reflected in higher prices for many months. Although the chart tells you the fact, whether price is really headed up or down, fundamental information about the commodity will help confirm or refute your analysis of the market.

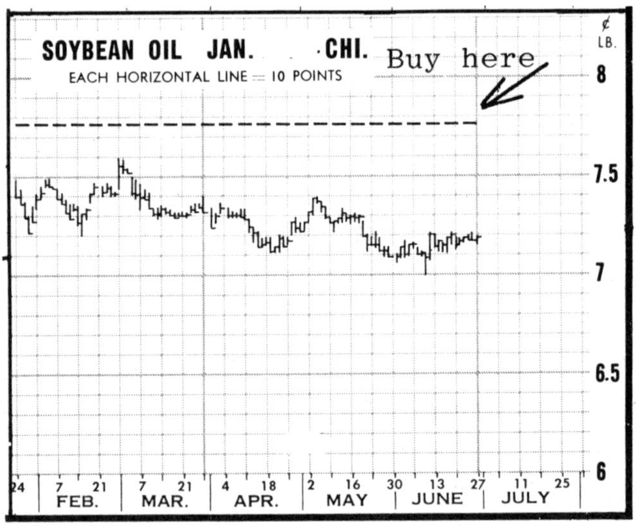

*Place your order to buy **above** the old range.*

Having once learned how to spot this type of market, the speculator must then decide at what point or price to buy or sell futures contracts. Many traders with a keen eye for chart patterns and market opportunities nonetheless suffer heavy losses from not knowing when and how to enter or exit the market. A calm, logical look at the graph for the commodity you wish to trade will usually give the answer. Don't forget, you want to let the market decide your position, because you can only profit by being with the market, not against it. To **buy** futures contracts during periods of advancing prices, place your orders **above** the previous trading range. To **sell** futures contracts during periods of declining prices, place your orders **below** the previous trading range.

In the case of January Soybean Oil, the trader expecting a rise in prices would want to place a buy order around 7.8¢, above the narrow trading range but not so far as to miss out on the bulk of a price rise.

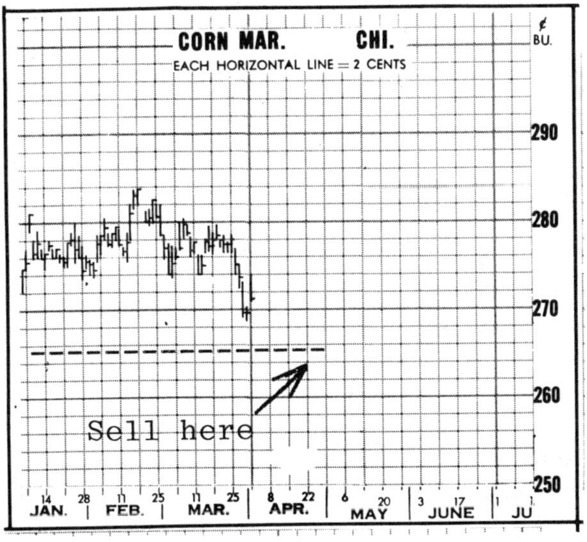

*Place your order to sell **below** the old range.*

In the case of March Corn, the trader who anticipates a huge new crop and a subsequent fall in prices will want to place a sell order around $2.65. Some traders would choose this point because its distance from the bottom of the former narrow trading range is equal to one-half the height (10¢) of the channel. Many other methods can be used for determining the exact level, but the rule is always "Buy above, sell below." If you had used this method to get into the March Corn contract, the result would have been very impressive indeed.

If you had sold at $2.65, and bought back after the reversal reached $2.10, the 55¢ profit would mean $2,750 per contract. With initial margin at $600, **profit would be 458%** (minus commission).

"But," you may well ask, "how do I know to get out at $2.10?" Novice traders will be surprised to learn that many speculators get wiped out because they don't know when to take their profits. I wish I had a nickel for every time a trader let substantial profits be erased by sitting through a complete reversal of a once-favorable price move, vainly hoping that yet another reversal will restore profits and add to them. Learning how to let your profits run, and then how to time your exit so as to take the bulk of those profits with you constitutes one of futures trading's finest arts.

Let us say that you have found the type of market you wish to trade. Prices have been wandering sideways in a narrow range and then moved out of that range, advancing or declining decidedly. Acting according to plan, you have taken a position in the market, buying if prices are rising and selling if prices are falling. You now hold real positions in the futures markets. Be forewarned. This is **not** the time to relax! The battle is only half over at this point, and the most dangerous moments in the life of the trade are still ahead. For you now have actual money at risk in the market, and you want to

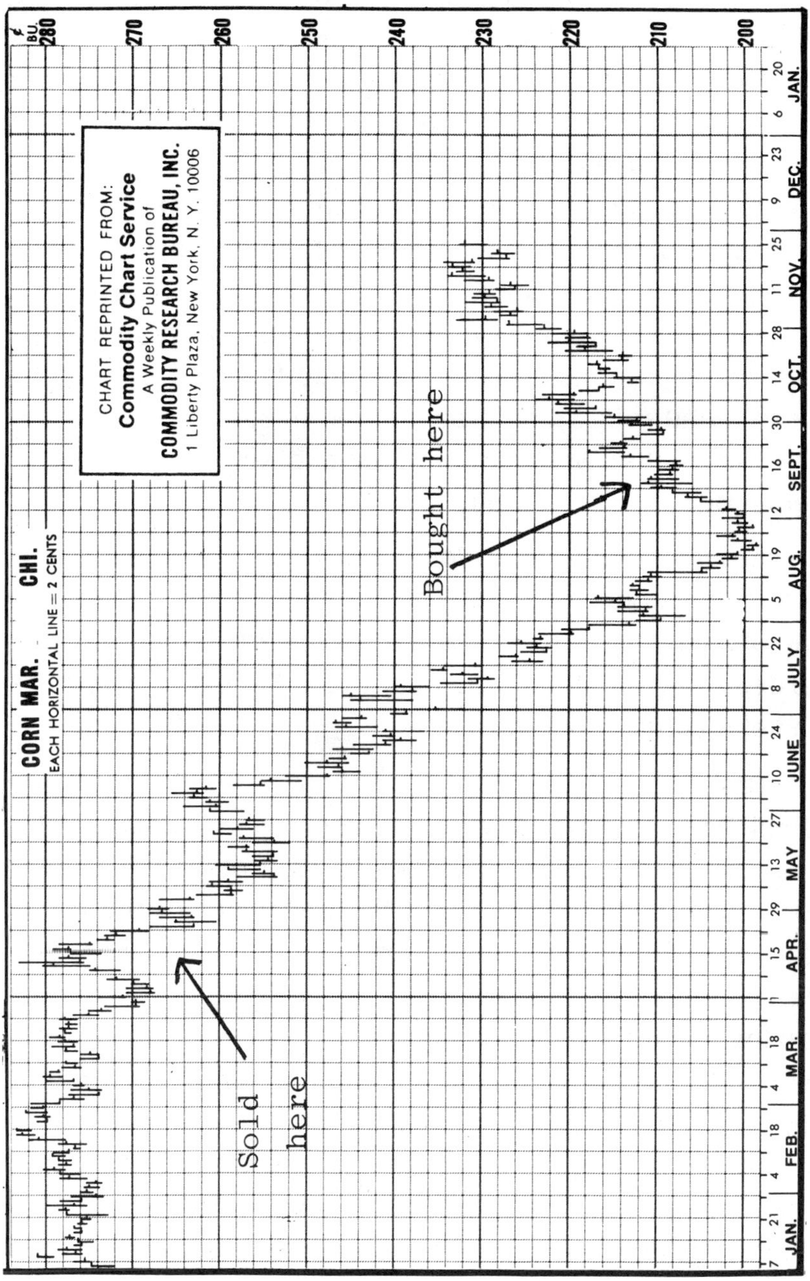
CORN MAR. CHI.
EACH HORIZONTAL LINE = 2 CENTS
¢ BU.
280
270
260
250
240
230
220
210
200
CHART REPRINTED FROM:
Commodity Chart Service
A Weekly Publication of
COMMODITY RESEARCH BUREAU, INC.
1 Liberty Plaza, New York, N. Y. 10006
Sold here
Bought here
JAN. FEB. MAR. APR. MAY JUNE JULY AUG. SEPT. OCT. NOV. DEC. JAN.

eventually get out of that market with a profit, or at least without having wrecked your commodity account.

The other half of the battle centers on one key decision: At what price do you wish to get out of the market? A method must be employed for determining at what price to liquidate the position, and an order formulated that will enable the pit trader to get you out when you want to get out, and at the price you want to get out at. At some time you will have to sell the contracts that you bought, or buy the contracts that you sold. In either case, you want to **buy low and sell high.** It doesn't matter in which order you do this, as long as you go with the market: you can buy low and sell high in a rising market or sell high and buy low in a declining market.

Whichever way it is done, the trader must decide the most reasonable and opportune moment for exiting from the market. Like the decision to enter the market in the first place, the decision to exit from the market can be determined by the market's actual price moves.

The first thing the speculator should do after establishing a commodity futures position is to enter a "stop-loss order." This order is designed to protect the position from ruinous losses by taking the trader out of the market when prices move adversely. When taking the initial position, the speculator may have used any number of orders to get into the market. One option would be the "stop" order, which rests until the price conditions match those of the order, at which time the "stop" is tripped and the order executed at the market. A "stop-loss" order is just like the normal "stop" order, except that instead of putting you into the market, it will take you out of the market. The stop-loss order instructs the broker to offset (get out of) the original market position once a certain price level has been reached. As the trader, **you** decide at what level that should be, and instruct the broker accordingly. The stop-loss order is planned and given to the broker either together with or immediately after the order that establishes the market position. A stop-loss will be of little use if formulated in haste when the market has already turned against the position.

Why is it called a "stop-loss"? The purpose of the order is to stop your losses at a predetermined, acceptable level, **before** they do irreparable harm to your commodity account. This puts into action the universal law of commodity futures trading: **Cut your losses short and let your profits run.** The stop-loss aids the trader in sticking to a disciplined, methodical plan for minimum losses and maximum profits. Before the trade has even been initiated, the computation of the stop-loss level lets the speculator decide exactly (give or take a small margin of error in actual execution) how much could be lost in the worst circumstance. The amount of money being risked is pin-pointed. The order tells the broker that you do not wish to lose more than $100 or $500 or whatever amount suits the trading plan. When things go wrong and the stop is tripped, the order will be executed at the "best possible" price available. **Caution:** In some cases, when prices are wildly fluctuating, it may not be possible to offset your market position through the use of a stop-loss order. Discuss this possibility **thoroughly** with your broker before investing any money in the market.

How would the "stop-loss" order be set by reference to price history and the price chart? In the cases of September Wheat and May Potatoes, the following graphs clearly suggest what action to take. After trading between $1.63 and $1.70 a bushel for nearly six months, the price of wheat rises to above $1.70 and heads for $1.75. The supply of wheat that has equalled demand and kept prices in a narrow range has evidently run out, and the squeeze has sent prices higher. The

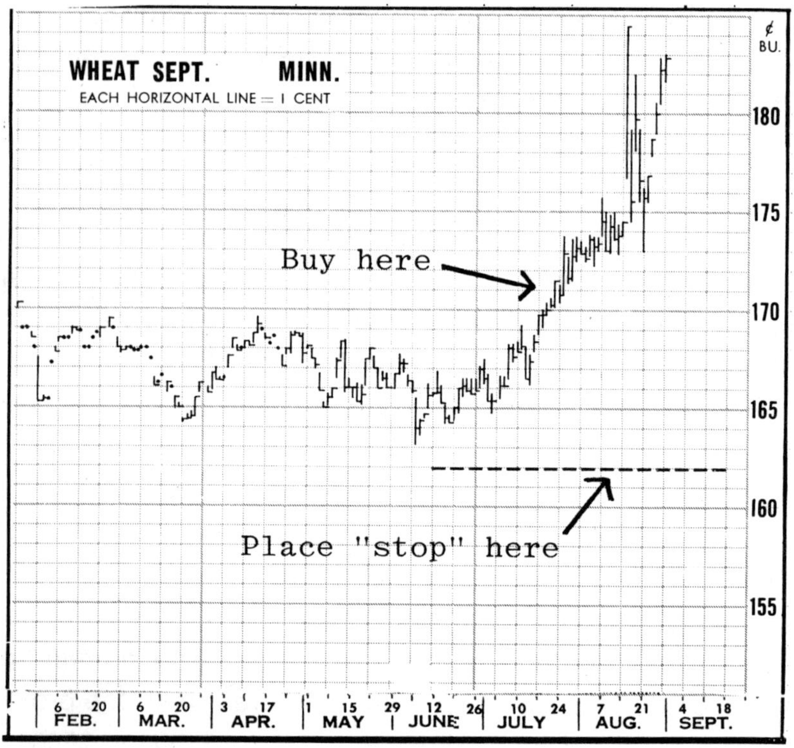
WHEAT SEPT. MINN.
EACH HORIZONTAL LINE = 1 CENT
Buy here
Place "stop" here
¢ BU.
180
175
170
165
160
155
FEB. MAR. APR. MAY JUNE JULY AUG. SEPT.

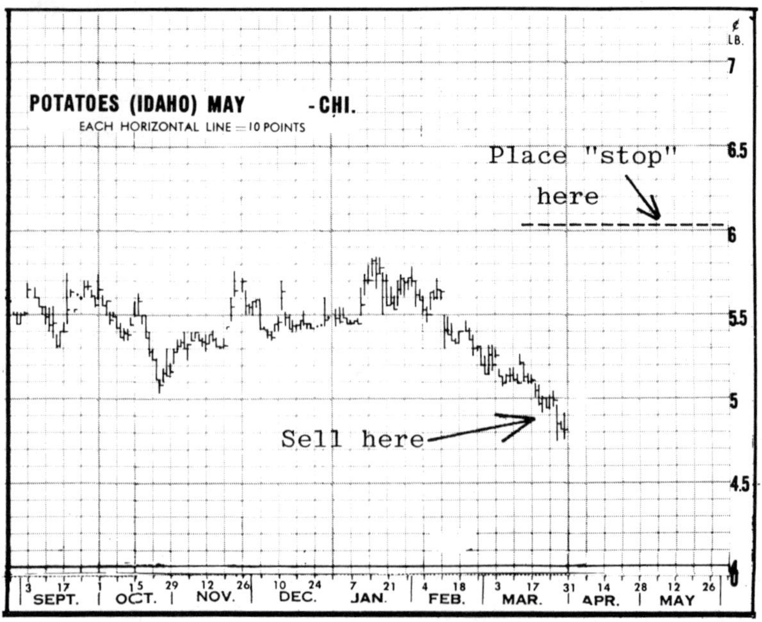
POTATOES (IDAHO) MAY -CHI.
EACH HORIZONTAL LINE = 10 POINTS
Place "stop" here
Sell here
¢ LB.
7
6.5
6
5.5
5
4.5
SEPT. OCT. NOV. DEC. JAN. FEB. MAR. APR. MAY

trader should buy wheat futures at $1.71 and place the protective stop-loss order on the other side of the trading range, at the $1.62 level or thereabouts. For potatoes, the price has fluctuated between 5¢ and 6¢ for eight solid months. It has now broken through the 5¢ barrier. Potato futures should be sold at the 4.9¢ level with a stop-loss entered at 6.1¢, above the trading range.

As you can see, a key location for your stop-loss is on the opposite side of the range in which prices previously traded. Normally, the likelihood of the price returning to the opposite side of its previous range, is not very great. However, there is **no** guarantee that price will not turn and strike into the other side of its former range.

If prices do return to the other side and you have placed your stop-loss order at that point, then you will suffer a loss, the size of which of course depends on how close to the range you set your stop. For the wheat contract, a reversal that tripped the stop at $1.62 would cost the trader 9¢ a bushel, or $450 per contract. Be **very careful** when using charts to set your stop-loss. Don't be fooled by the increments of the chart's construction into thinking that a small move on the chart equals a small loss. How much would you lose, for example, if you were "stopped out" of the October Cotton contract?

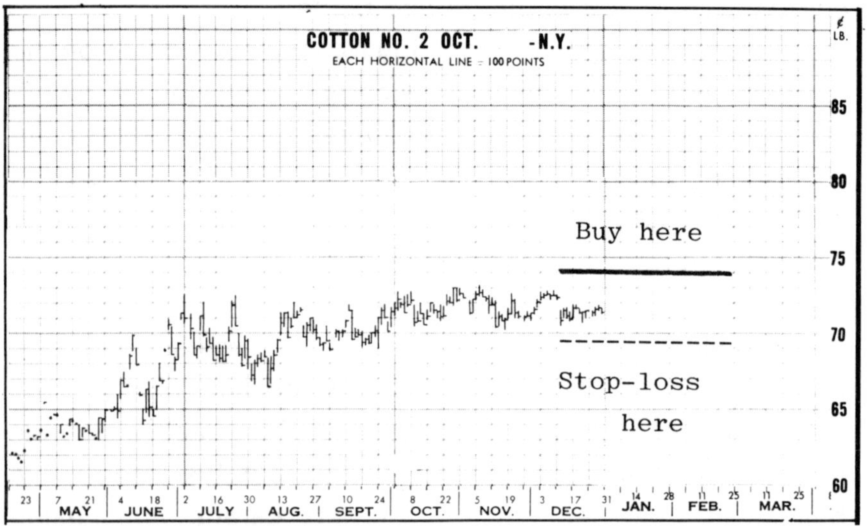

Suppose that you are planning to buy cotton when the price breaks upward out of its 3 month range of 3¢, from 70.5¢ to 73¢. You anticipate going long at 74¢, and place your stop-order to buy at that level. Next you set your stop-loss below the previous range, at 69.5¢. Your order limits your loss-risk to 4.5¢, a very small move on the cotton chart. But what does this short distance, those few pennies, translate into per contract? Our "Trading Facts" tell us that every 1¢ move in cotton is worth $500 per contract. The amount being risked here, despite appearances, is a whopping $2,225.

In most circumstances, placing the stop-loss order on the opposite side of the trading range provides the best protection in the best location until prices start moving in a favorable direction. Whether or not the trader can afford to follow the rule, as in the case of cotton, will depend on the amount of capital available for risk. If you can't afford to set your stop-loss at such a distance from the established position, then the market is too volatile for you to trade, no matter what the chart looks like.

If you have set your stop-loss, and prices continue to move in your favor, the distance between the stop-loss and the current price will increase. Your profits will be increasing, but your level of protection will be going nowhere. The solution is to move your stop-loss order in the same direction as the favorable price move, keeping the distance between the stop and current prices about the same as the original difference between the price of the established position and the level of the stop. Then, when prices do finally turn, you will be taken out of the market with most of your profits intact, having paid a small, predetermined amount for the privilege of riding the price move as far as the market would go.

This movement of stop-loss orders is in reaction to a new problem. The preceding illustrations were centered around protecting the commodity futures position when the market made an adverse move. We wanted to limit our losses to a preset amount in case our price forecasts were wrong. Now we face the "problem" most traders rarely get a chance to solve: "Where and when do I get out with my profits?" What do you do when you have a profit and at what price do you get out and take that profit? Strangely enough, this can be a more difficult predicament than that of deciding when to cut your losses short. If your stop-loss is set, it will take you out of a losing market quickly, without hesitation. But if profits are piling up, what signal tells the trader its time to take the money and run?

Suppose, for example, that you have a $1,000 profit on your commodity position. Should you stay with the position, hoping your profits will increase, or get out while the getting is good? Many speculators find this the hardest question to face in futures trading. If the market reverses itself, then the $1,000 profit disappears or perhaps turns into a $1,000 loss for the trader who chose to stay in. However, if you do get out, and then the market keeps moving until your profits would have been $10,000, you will feel sick about liquidating so early. The best rule for offsetting or getting out of profitable commodity futures positions is the method known as the "trailing stop."

Once more, the price chart aids us in demonstrating the principle of the trailing stop. As with the stop-loss order, the chart serves as a handy visual guide to where and when to act. The cotton market shown in the December Cotton graph qualified for trading once prices settled into a lengthy sideways channel in the early summer months. Prices moved out of that range when demand achieved a dominance over supply, pushing prices upward and into a steady climb. When was the time to buy? Once prices penetrated the old ceiling, the trader could have been on board the big move with a stop order to buy at 30¢. The first stop-loss is placed at level S_1 — 27¢. This would be below the old trading range of 27.8¢ to 29.8¢. If the price of the December Cotton contract declined to level S_1 shortly after the position was established at 30¢, the trader would lose $1,500, an amount determined beforehand as an acceptable degree of loss. But as we would expect in this kind of market, cotton prices continued their upward trend.

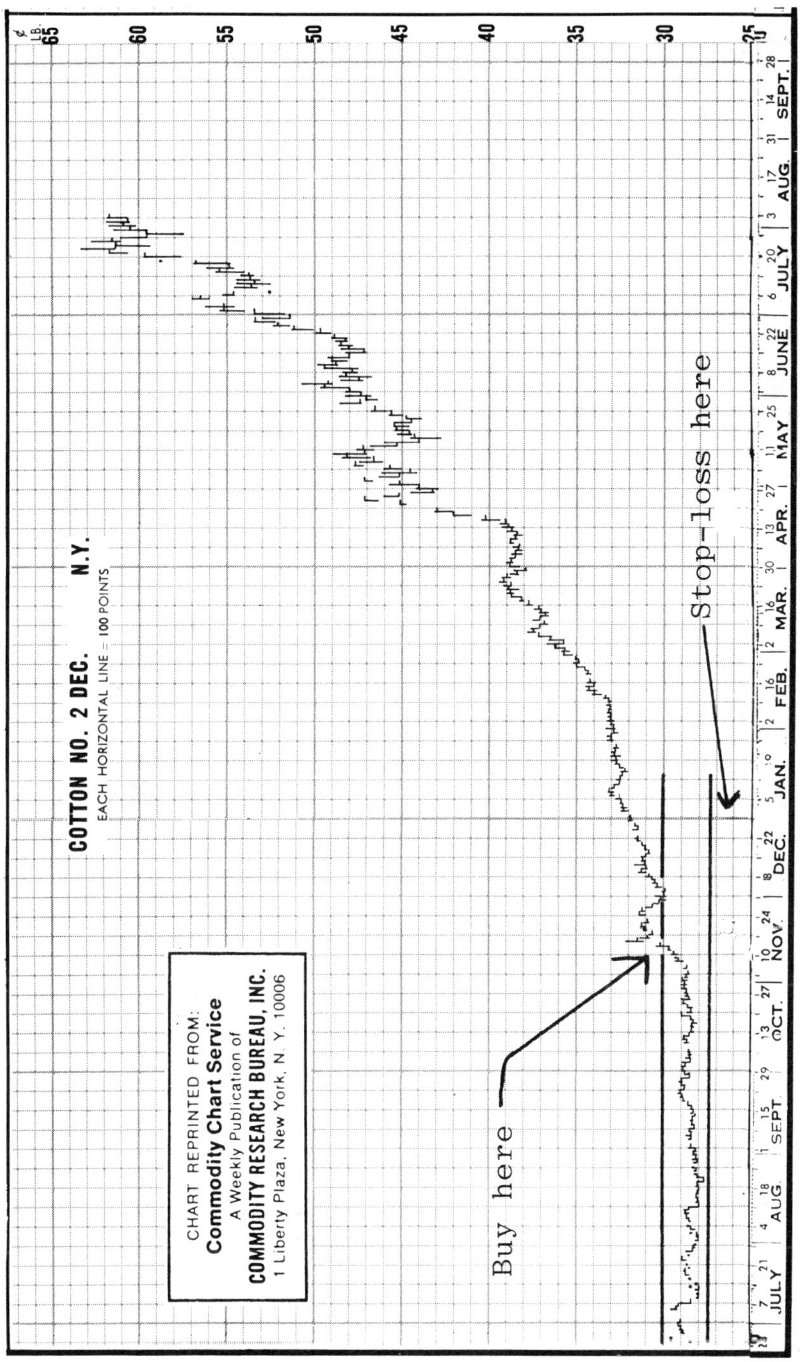
COTTON NO. 2 DEC. N.Y.
EACH HORIZONTAL LINE = 100 POINTS
CHART REPRINTED FROM:
Commodity Chart Service
A Weekly Publication of
COMMODITY RESEARCH BUREAU, INC.
1 Liberty Plaza, New York, N. Y. 10006
Buy here
Stop-loss here

After prices have advanced to the point where the trader has broken even on the margin deposit, or scored a significant paper profit, the stop-loss level can be raised. Let us say that December Cotton has hit 33¢. You move your stop-loss up to S_2 — 30¢. Then, if prices had suddenly turned downward and tripped your stop-loss, the position would be closed without gain or loss (except for commission costs). Cotton prices, however, kept going up. When the futures price passes through 37¢, the stop-loss is raised once more, this time to S_3 — 33¢. Now if you are "stopped out," a profit of $1,500 is assured. When prices hit 47¢, you again move the stop up, to S_4 at 37¢, now allowing a bit more cushion on the downside in respect for an increasingly volatile market (and because a good stock of paper profits covers the risk).

As prices shoot up beyond 55¢, the stop-loss is moved up to S_5 at 47¢, and the process is repeated at predetermined steps so long as the price line continues to rise. Finally, you are stopped out by a large reversal to S_8 at 77¢. The stops have been "trailed" behind the price action, keeping you in the market as long as the trend continued, but taking you out of the marekt when it firmly decides to head in an adverse direction.

There is no hard and fast rule dictating just how far below current prices the stop-loss order should be trailed. The trader who moved the stop-loss from S_1 to S_2 when prices hit 33¢ was playing a conservative, close stop-loss game. A reversal at that moment would have wiped out the position without a loss, it is true, but it also would have meant missing out on the big move upward if it resumed. Another trader might have left the stop-loss order at S_1 until prices passed through 37¢, and then moved the stop-loss up directly to S_3. Many traders using stops could have been stopped out by the temproary 6¢ reversal in May, while others with stops set farther away

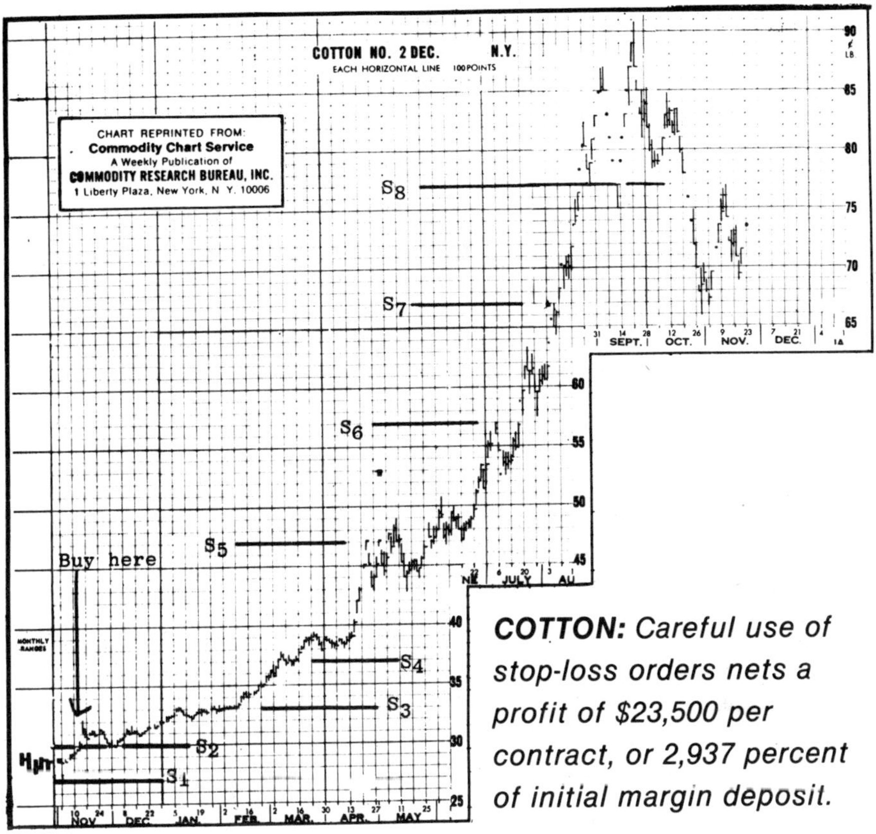

COTTON: *Careful use of stop-loss orders nets a profit of $23,500 per contract, or 2,937 percent of initial margin deposit.*

TRAIL YOUR STOP-LOSS ORDERS TO PROTECT PROFITS

stayed in the game. On the other hand, traders who set their stops fairly close would have gotten out of the market far more quickly, and with more profits intact, in October than would have those speculators with distant stops at 70¢ or 65¢. Setting stop-loss points is an art that requires practice and precision. The **general rule** is to trail the stops far enough below or above the current market prices so that minor fluctuations will not result in an offsetting of the position and yet close enough so that when the market does actually reverse its price direction, the trader is taken out with a substantial profit still intact.

At level S_8, the stop-loss is tripped when the market makes a big decline after hitting the top of its long advance. Let's say your futures contract, bought at 30¢, is sold at 77¢. Your profit per contract is 47¢, with each 1¢ move equalling $500. In this example, the initial investment required for one cotton futures contract was $800. Your total per contract **profit was $23,500 or 2,937 percent** of invested capital. This astonishing return on a very small amount of investment capital was realized in a mere seven months' time. Only two market decisions were required of the trader:

1. Futures contracts had to be bought when prices were seen to advance out of a narrow trading range.

2. "Stops" had to be trailed below the price advance, being kept far enough away from current prices so that a minor fluctuation did not take the trader out of the market, but close enough so that a major price reversal automatically liquidated the position.

The speculator in December Cotton had a relatively easy time of it. There was little to do but follow the market's decisions, buying when the market rose and selling when it turned. No wonder so many investors are finding commodity futures trading so appealing.

The examples cited up to this point were not rare, isolated cases. Price fluctuations such as those illustrated so far occur often enough to assure the patient speculator of several rich opportunities each year. In the following pages we will take a look at a 12 year period from 1968-1980, examining actual markets that could have been traded (and were traded by many) for very sizable returns. We look to the pages of history because here history is our best teacher. It confirms the soundness of the method and the practicality of its application. By studying the markets of the past, you will learn how to take positions in the same type of market when it occurs in the future. And you may rest assured that this type of market **will be repeated** as long as there are futures markets. From 1980 to 1990 to 2000 and beyond, there will be price fluctuations in one commodity or another which substantially qualify for the method of trading under discussion here. Anyone with modest amounts of risk capital and possessing average intelligence should be able to realize significant profits from a majority of these opportunities.

A commodity futures contract comes naked into the world. It springs up ready to trade, lives tumultuously for a year or so, and then dies into history. Thousands and thousands of contracts in dozens of commodities have come and gone in this way, leaving a rich record of lessons for the prospective commodity futures trader. These are the lessons from which we hope to profit. We have learned already the major principles: buy in an advancing market, sell in a declining market, and stay out of the market altogether when the price is wandering aimlessly sideways. In trading commodity futures, you are really taking positions in relationship to "price patterns" — advancing patterns, declining patterns, sideways patterns, — that are formed by the life and death of the futures contract. These patterns are

Each futures contract comes naked into the world. Its trading life fills the blank space of the price chart. As the year unfolds, price can only go sideways, up, or down. Every year, contracts start anew. Every year, some commodity chart will form the simple pattern of channels and breakouts offering profits to the trader the histories of the contracts. Remember the old saying: "Those who don't understand the lessons of history are bound to repeat the mistakes of history."

As Harry Truman put it:

> *"There is nothing new under the sun. If it is happening today, it has happened in the past. For the solutions to today's opportunities — look to your history books."*

The history books of the commodity futures markets are made up of the charts and graphs you will be examining shortly. These unfold what **actually** happened in the past to the price of various commodities. Whatever interests you — wheat, corn, soybeans, beef, hogs, cotton, sugar, lumber, orange juice, gold, Treasury Bills, et. al. — history reveals the method for trading your chosen commodity successfully.

* * * * * * * * * * * * * * * *

Were there any futures markets in 1968 that showed the simple price pattern we have been studying? Did the pattern reoccur in 1969? Would our method have yielded profits in 1970? Could you have made a fortune in 1975? 1980? Will there be potential trading bonanzas in 1990? 2000? We can answer these questions by looking at some actual case histories, beginning with the period from 1968 through 1972. Remember: these are **not** hypothetical examples. These charts record the real price activity of real commodity markets. The profits earned in these markets were very real profits. Look through this period of history carefully on your own, before reading the commentary that follows. As you examine the charts, recall the principles outlined so far in this book and the trading methods you have learned.

In each case, ask yourself: "How would **I** have traded this market?" Inspecting the charts, determine for yourself the following:

1 .At which point should you have bought?

2 .At which point should you have sold?

3 .Where should your stop-loss have been placed?

4 .How much could **you** have earned by trading these markets?

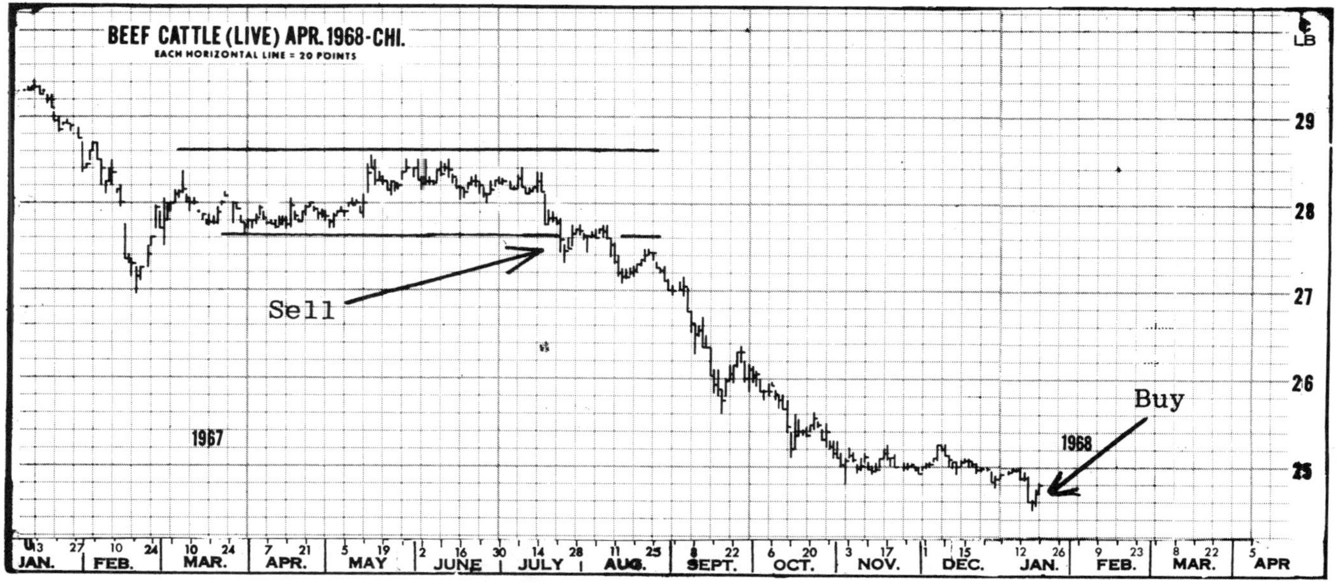

CATTLE: *PROFIT WAS 300% IN SIX MONTHS.*

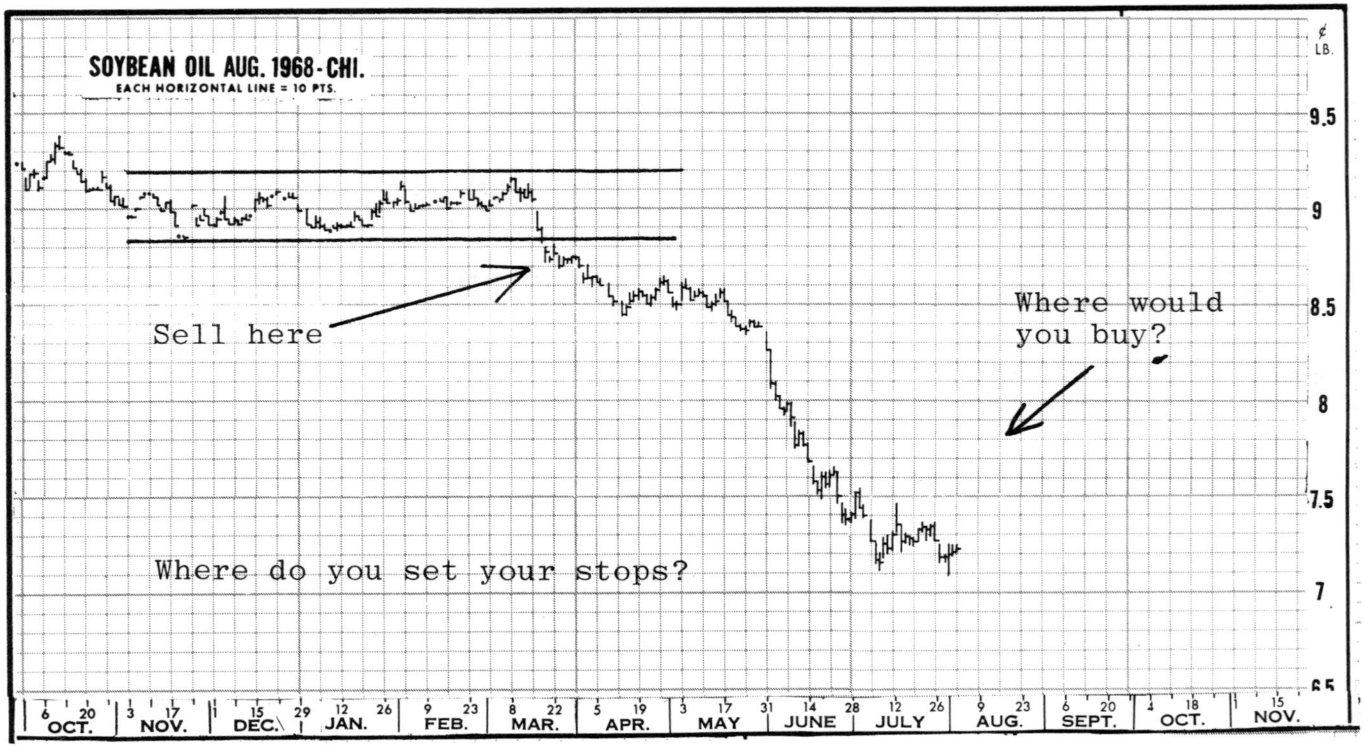

SOYBEAN OIL: *A 300 PERCENT RETURN ON INITIAL MARGIN.*

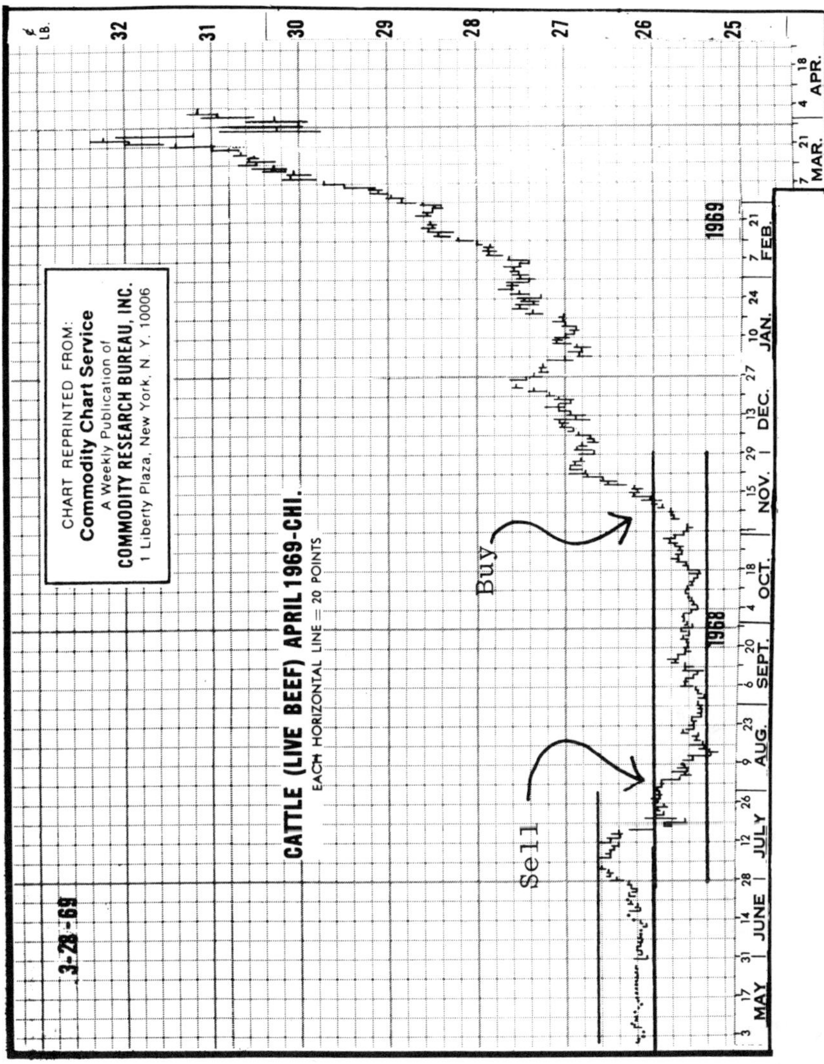

CATTLE: *GO WHERE THE MARKET GOES.*

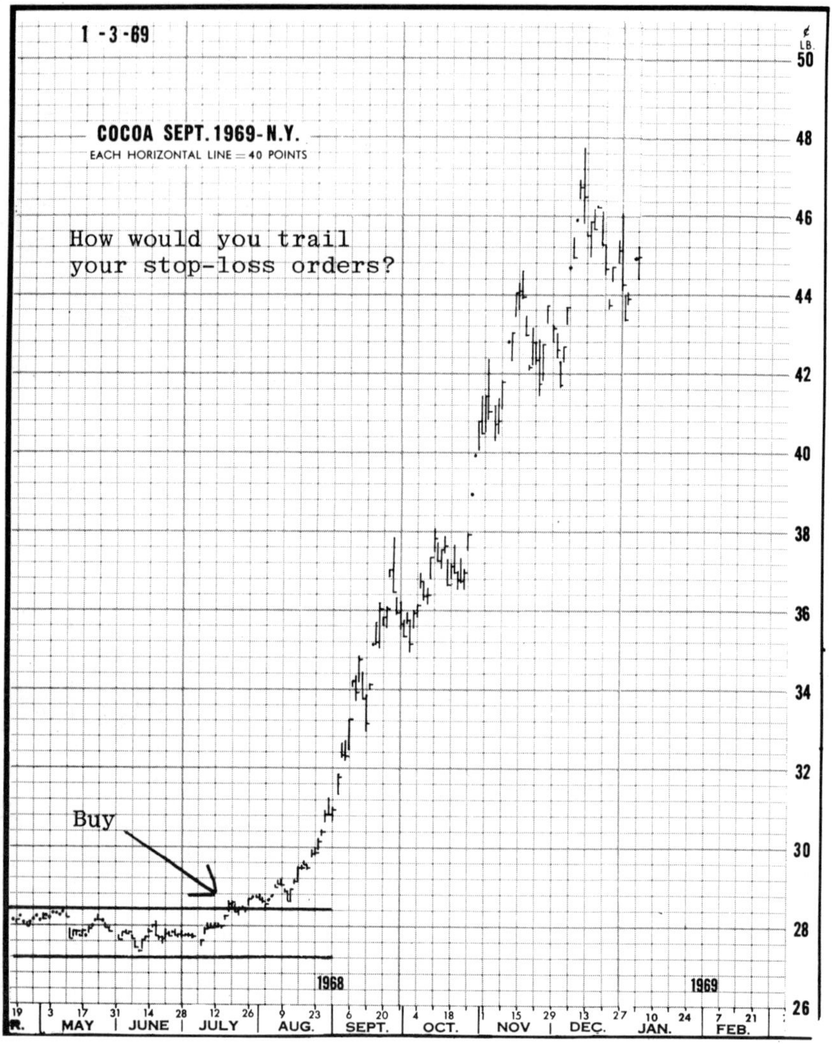

COCOA: *$5,400 PROFIT PER CONTRACT, OR 1,080 PERCENT OF INVESTED CAPITAL.*

RAPESEED: *PROFIT PER CONTRACT WAS $3,250, OR 650 PERCENT.*

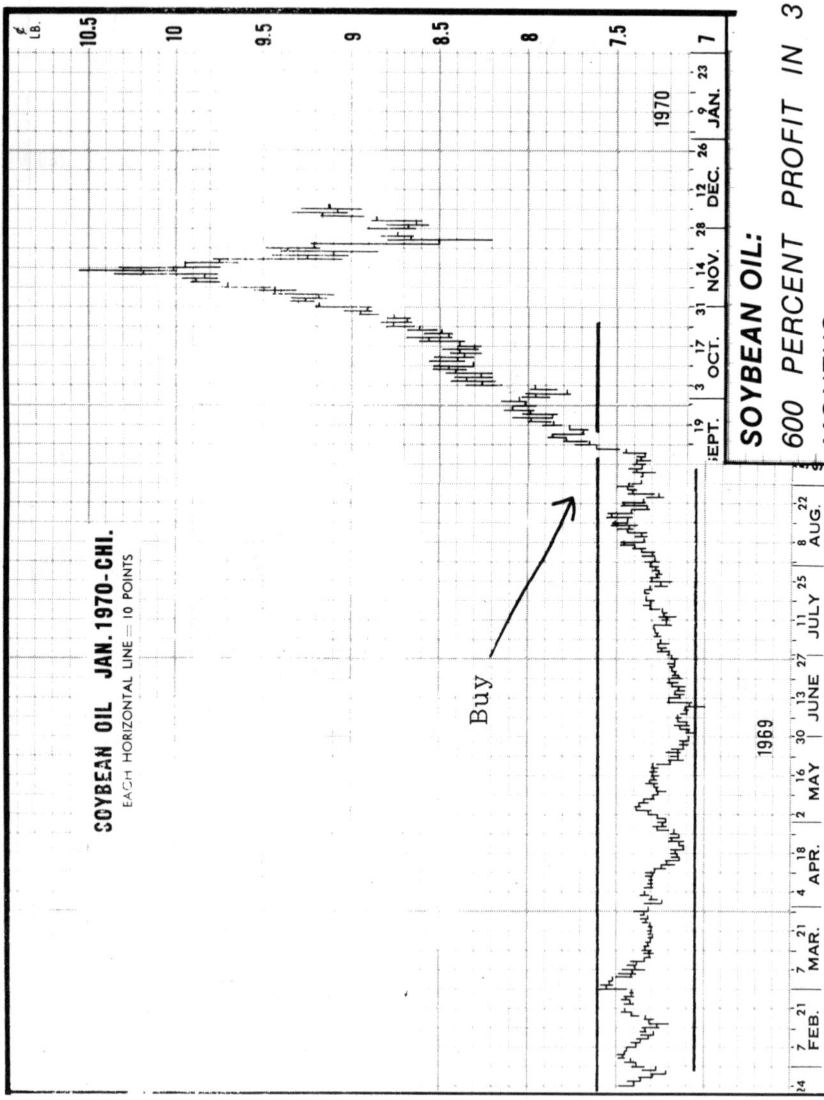

SOYBEAN OIL:
600 PERCENT PROFIT IN 3 MONTHS.

SOYBEAN OIL: *OIL KEEPS ON GOING UP. PROFIT WAS $3,720 PER CONTRACT.*

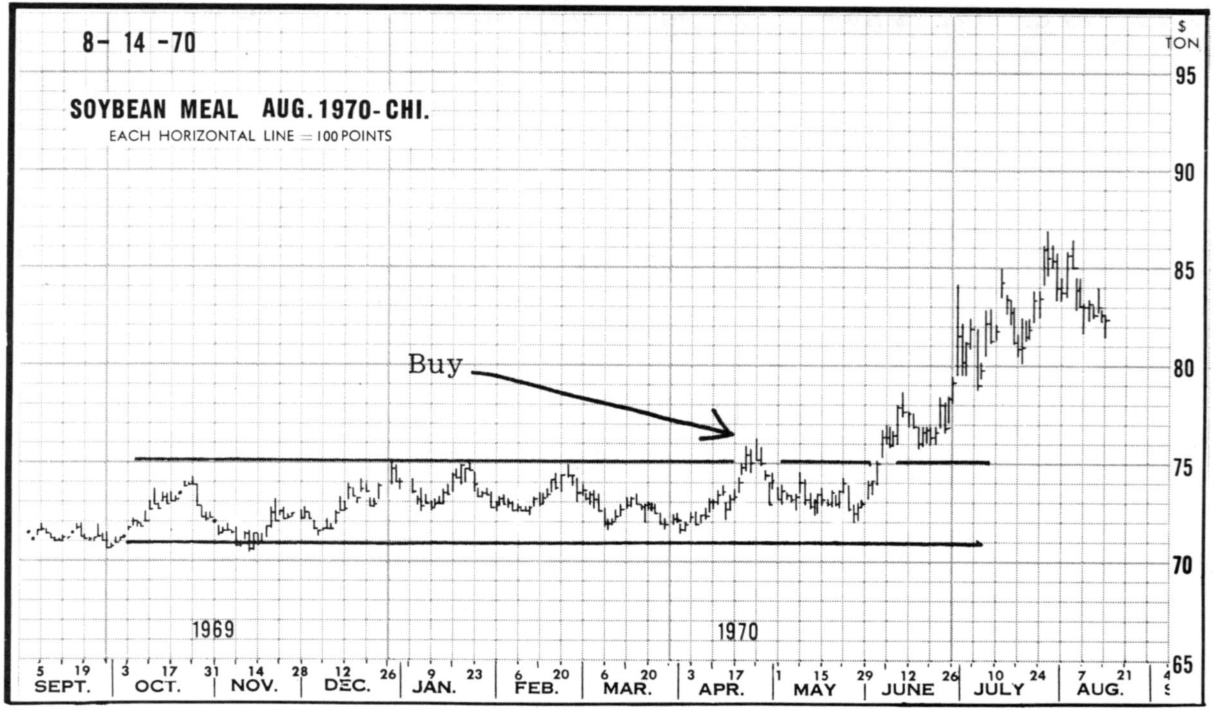

SOYBEAN MEAL: *MEAL AND OIL MAKE RELATED MOVES. PROFIT: $1,000 PER CONTRACT, OR 333 PERCENT.*

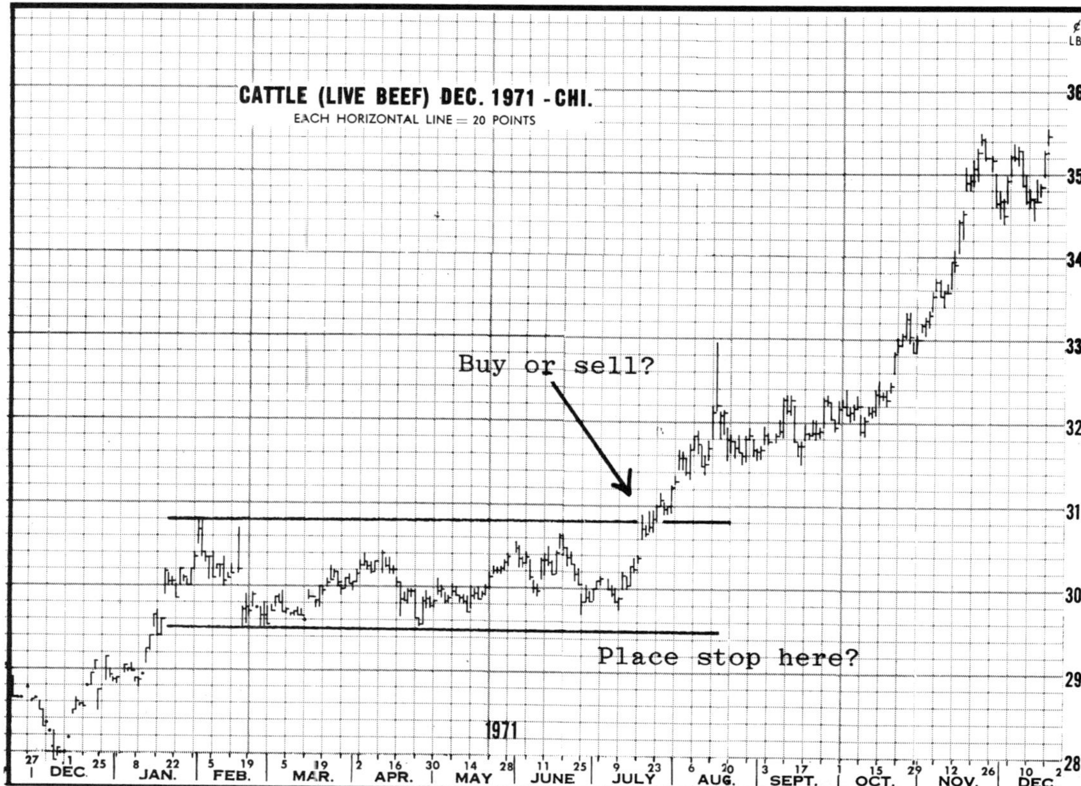

CATTLE: *POTENTIAL PROFIT, ON A MARGIN OF $400, WAS $1,600.*

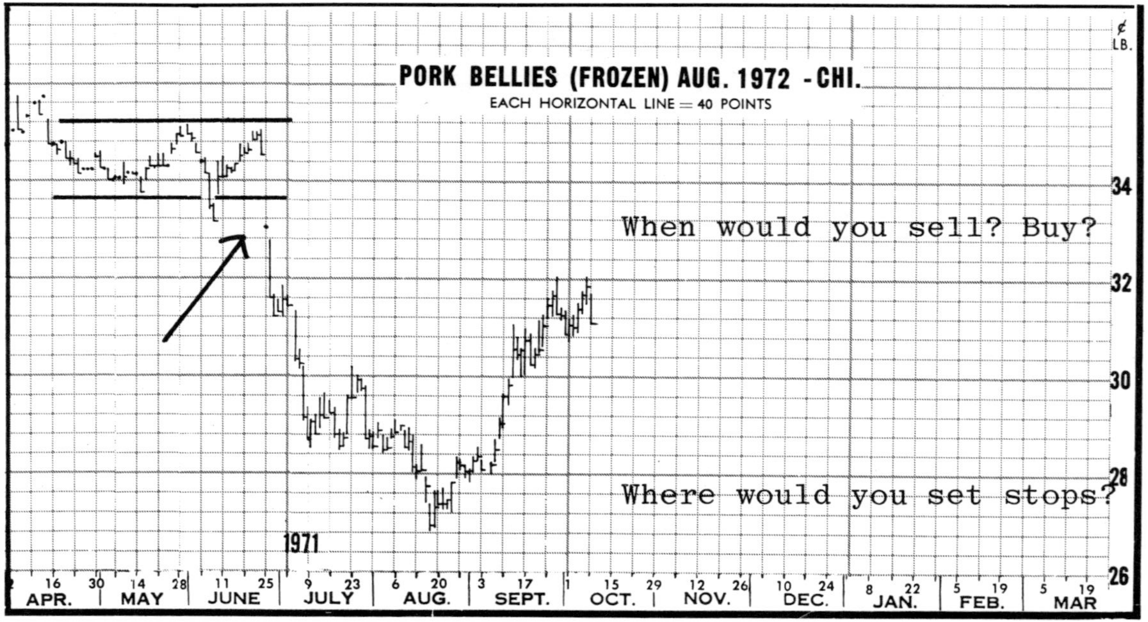

PORK BELLIES: *BELLIES AND CATTLE CAN MOVE IN OPPOSITE DIRECTIONS. PROFIT IN BELLIES ON THE SHORT SIDE WAS $2,160 PER CONTRACT, OR 360 PERCENT.*

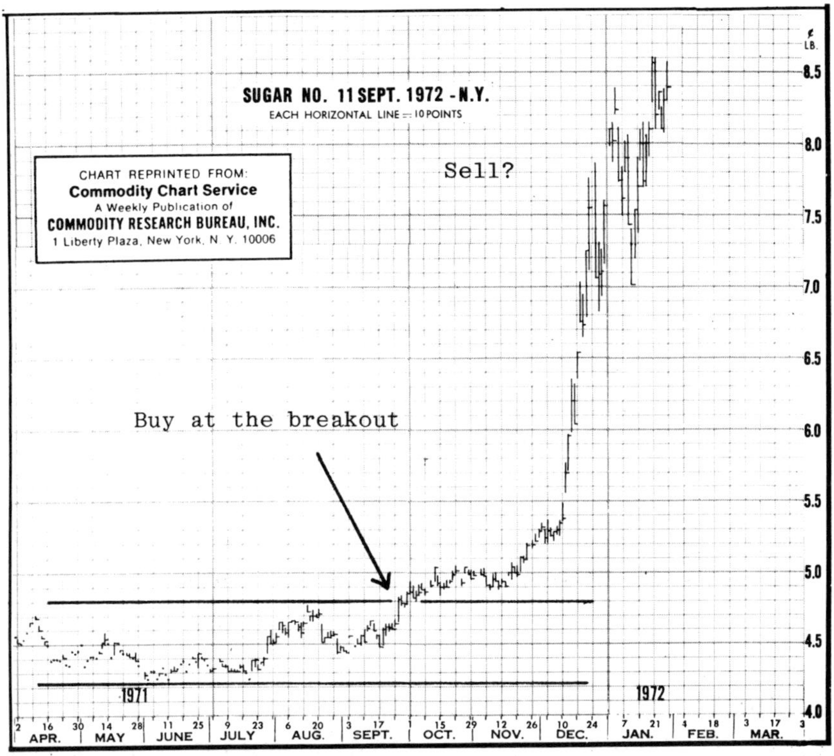

SUGAR: *PRICES DOUBLE IN SIX MONTHS. PROFITS ON THE LONG SIDE WERE $4,256 PER CONTRACT.*

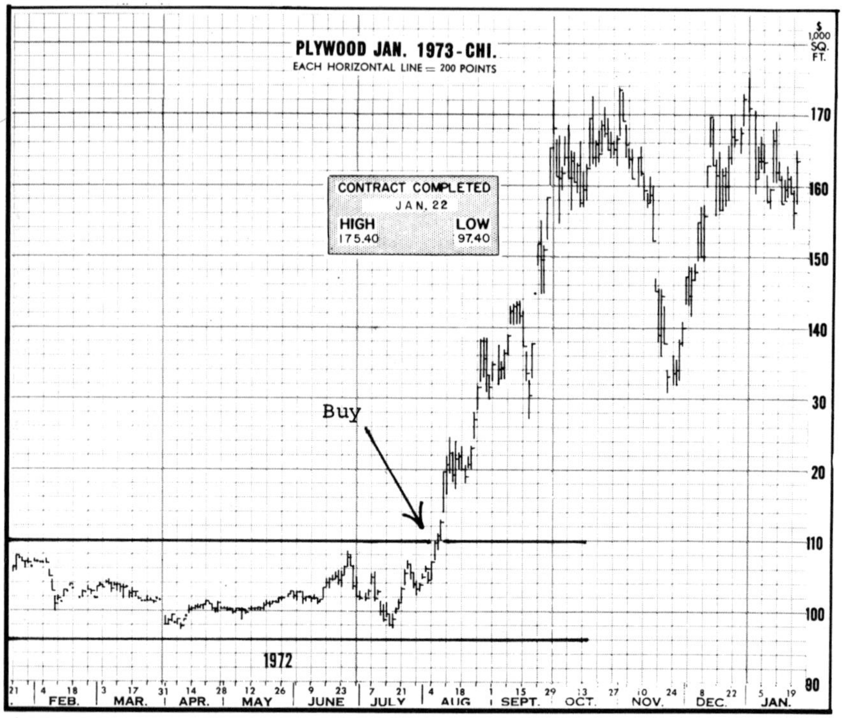

CALCULATE FOR YOURSELF THE PROFIT IN PLYWOOD. EVERY $1 MOVE EQUALS $76.03. WOULD YOU HAVE CAUGHT THE MOVE?

COMMENTARY: 1968 through 1972

Our travels through history begin with the April 1968 Live Beef Cattle futures contract. For nearly 18 weeks in 1967 the price of the April 1968 contract hovered between 27.5 and 28.5 cents a pound. In mid-July, however, prices declined out of this narrow range. This was one time in history when beef prices were not constantly going up. When prices declined below 27.5 cents a pound, one futures contract could have been sold. The stop-loss order could have been placed above the trading range, around 28.75 or 29 cents. Once prices gathered the force to break out below the old channel, the big drop began and prices never rose back anywhere near their former norm. If the specualtor sold at 27.5 cents and liquidated when prices hit 25 cents in mid-November, the profit for each $400 in margin would have been $1000 — a return of 250% in four months.

The soybean oil market for 1968 is another example of how, incredible as it may seem, you can make handsome profits when prices go down. From late October to the middle of March, the price for the August 1968 contract stuck to the range between 8.8 and 9.2 cents per pound. Then an abnormally sharp move pushed the price below the old price floor. The market clearly signalled the methodical trader to sell at 8.7, with a stop-loss set around 9.2. After hesitating at the 8.6 level for another month, prices failed to rally back anywhere close to the old range (or the speculator's stop) and the collapse began in earnest. If you had bought back when prices leveled off at 7.2, the profit per contract would have been $900, a 300 percent return on the initial margin of $300.

Of course history also tells us what happens to price over the long run. How much is soybean oil going for today? By 1980 the cash price of soybean oil was ranging between 20 and 27 cents a pound. Why? Once again, demand and supply. Take a look at the list of ingredients in your salad oil, margarine, or any of a dozen products containing vegetable oil. Chances are the main ingredient is soybean oil. Soybean oil and its two cousins in the soy complex, soybeans and soybean meal, have enjoyed enormous growth in popularity since the 1960s. These three items now form an integral part of the agriculture and food production systems, both in the United States and abroad. Their importance is reflected in their price, and the three often move together in parallel directions on the price charts.

Cattle and soybean oil were not the only commodities to qualify for trading by our method during 1968. Other possibilities included futures contracts in barley, corn, live hogs, oats, platinum, propane, rapeseed, soybean meal, and wheat. But let us turn now to 1969 when rising prices in a number of commodities offered great trading situations.

The April 1969 Live Beef Cattle contract presents an especially interesting case study. Here we find **two** narrow trading ranges and **two** price breakouts, one down and one up. From May to mid-July prices hold tight to the range between 26 and 26.6. When prices head below 26 cents, our speculator naturally sells. Only this time the force is not enough to inspire a long downtrend. Prices are already near their historic lows, and a new channel begins to form. By the first week in September, the trader has held the "short" position for more than a month, and watched prices level out, and then begin to creep upward. Since there is no wisdom in hanging on to a position that won't move favorably, the trader gets out with a small profit, and awaits a new signal from the market.

That signal comes on November 14, when prices tire of their old low channel and start their steady climb upward. Now was a very good time to buy. The supply of cheap beef had finally been exhausted, herds reduced and inventories depleted, until prices had no choice but to rise, and rise substantially. Even though shoppers were complaining about the price of beef in the supermarkets, their complaints could have no persuasive effect on the workings of the market. A better solution for the frustrated consumer would be a profitable long position in the futures market. A contract purchased at 26¢ a pound and sold at 30¢ a pound would have meant a $1,600 profit for each $400 invested. The rate of return was 400 percent in five months time. You can buy a lot of steaks with that.

The September 1969 Cocoa futures contract was another spectacular winner. The price remained near 28¢ a pound for nearly four months. Then it advanced to 29¢, 30¢, 31¢, and so on all the way up to nearly 48¢ a pound. Getting on board the cocoa express entailed no more than charting the trading channel, and acting when prices went through the ceiling at 28¢. The trader who bought at that point could watch the profits roll up effortlessly until prices grew volatile near 36¢. But a stop-loss properly trailed 1.4 or 1.8 cents behind the previous day's close would never have caused the position to be liquidated, and the trader could safely continue the climb up. If the position were closed out at 46¢, after the big one day rise and fall toward 48¢, the profit would have been $5,400 on an initial margin of $500, a return of 1,080 percent in less than six months time.

Futures contracts for rapeseed trade on the Winnipeg Commodity Exchange in Canada. Rapeseed itself is about half the size of a "bb pellet" and deep brown in color, sometimes nearly reddish. It grows like wheat and is harvested each year across the plains of Canada. Crushed, the seed produces an oil used in the production of rayon and acetate, or for human consumption as a substitute for olive and soybean oil. While very little rapeseed is grown in the U.S., this commodity is an important crop for Canada, China, France, India, and Poland.

Trading the Canadian rapeseed market of 1969 demonstrated the life-saving value of the method we have been exploring. Rapeseed traded between $2.02 and $2.10 for four straight months. In July the price broke upward out of the channel, and the speculator bought at $2.12. The stop-loss order would be placed just below $2.00. Here you will note that prices subsequently declined to a level dangerously close to the "stop." But this time the trader stayed in, and waited. Why? First of all, discipline. The method determined a stop-loss just below $2.00. The wise trader won't second guess the method. Second, the trader had an idea about **why** prices were declining. There is traditionally a weakness in grain prices at some point early in the summer months, after harvests and before winter shortages. This could easily be discovered by a quick look at previous price charts and records. Sure enough, the price advance resumed in September until this humble seed was a star performer. Margin on the (then) 5,000 bushel contract was $500. If the long position were sold off at $2.75, profit per contract would be $3,250 or 650 percent.

1970 was once more a good year for speculating in the soybean complex, only this time the price direction was up. The charts for soybean meal and soybean oil both reveal similar price patterns and profit opportunities. When the soybeans have been crushed by the processor, the meal and oil produced represent the real value and most popular markets; soybeans themselves are comparatively useless. The modern demand for soybean production can only partially be explained by the widespread use of soybean oil. Just as important is the growing demand for soybean meal. This meal is one of the most protein rich foods available in the world, running as high as 50 percent protein. Ranchers discovered its great value as an element in livestock feed, so that now the demand for soybean meal (and thus the price fluctuations of meal, beans, and oil) depends in significant part on the state of the livestock industry (and thus on the price fluctuations of cattle, hogs, and poultry). Meal has also become an increasingly utilized filler in human food products, especially as a meat supplement or substitute.

The first opportunity actually came in soybean oil in late 1969, when the January contract burst out of its 7 month long channel. This represented a profit of $1,800 per contract, on a margin of $300, a return of 600 percent. The January contract had hit its high on November 13th, 1969. At that time, the October 1970 contract lagged well behind, as distant contracts usually do (obviously immediate supply and demand pressures have more influence on the price of contracts soon to be deliverable than on contracts falling due many months later). October oil made only a small peak in November, and then continued to rest in a narrow range until February of 1970. The demand for oil evidently lost none of its strength, and carried the October contract sharply and steadily to new highs. This time maximum profits per contract were $3,720, or 800 percent. Thus using the method we have discussed, you could have profited **twice,** in the space of a year, from what was essentially the same price move in soybean oil, just by charting both the nearby and the distant contracts.

Knowing that the price moves of soybean meal often parallel those of soybean oil, our trader was also charting meal contracts in this period. Sure enough, a lengthy channel formed throughout late 1969 and into 1970. As the August Soybean Meal contract drew within a few months of delivery, the same demand pressure pushing soybean oil prices up did its work on meal. Here the profit opportunity was $1,000 per contract, a 333 percent return on the $300 margin.

1971 presented contrasting opportunities in the livestock contracts. Once more beef prices started a strong ascent, possibly as a result of the "cattle cycle" as producers take a number of years to reduce (or build) their herds in response to price trends. Where would you have bought? Sold? Would you have been stopped out in September? Potential profit was, at a margin of $400, 400 percent at $1,600 per contract.

August 1972 Pork Bellies tell a different tale. While an apparent shortage of cheap beef was driving cattle prices up, pork prices crashed, probably reflecting abundant stocks built up during the period of low, stable beef prices. The consumer will quickly switch back and forth between pork and beef in response to changes in their price differential, so that traders in cattle follow actions in the pork markets, and vice versa. Pork bellies, the underside of the hog from which bacon is made, declined in price. The trader could have sold on the first descent through the 33.6¢ level, placed a stop-loss order at 35.6 or 36¢. Were the contract liquidated (bought) at 27.6¢, profit would have been $2,160 per contract, 360 percent of the initial $600 margin.

1972 brought many substantial market moves in the pattern we have isolated. These included futures contracts in oats, palladium, live beef cattle, cotton, silver coins, platinum, barley, soybean meal, plywood, sugar, the British Pound and wheat. Most of these commodities advanced in price, some spectacularly so. Thus 1972 was a **bad year** for the consumer, but a **good** year for the commodity futures trader. To the futures speculator, it makes no difference whether prices advance or decline. The trader who is correctly positioned can profit either way. All that is required is that prices do move — up or down — and the profit potential appears. While shoppers lament the high cost of living and Congress puzzles over economic policy, you can be acting, and smiling at the results. Up or down, the commodity speculator knows that price moves mean an exceptional opportunity for investment profit and a unique method for offsetting the high cost of retail goods and services.

Sugar frequently turns up in our reviews of big winners. The September 1972 futures contract shows prices **doubling** from April of 1971 to January of 1972. The breakout from the old channel came in early October. After a month of testing the waters, prices could not be forced back and the way was open for a gigantic leap. Profit per contract according to the method: $4,256 in four months. The jump in January Plywood was similarly extreme. Calculate for yourself the profit easily available to the speculator in plywood, and you'll know why so many people are now getting into commodity trading.

* * * * * * * * * * * * * * * * * * *

You have now taken a close look at a dozen historical examples demonstrating how one trading technique can bring you astonishing profits in the futures markets. By this time, you should be able to tell quickly, by a glance at the price chart, whether a futures contract qualifies for successful method trading. You should also know now how to pick your buy and sell points, and how to set your stop-loss order. Turning to the years from 1973 through 1976, apply the tools and skills you have developed. Treat each example as if it were happening **today,** for these patterns and opportunities will repeat themselves indefinitely in the future. These were some of the most exciting, fabulously profitable years in recent futures trading history. Where would **you** stand financially today if you had been trading these markets?

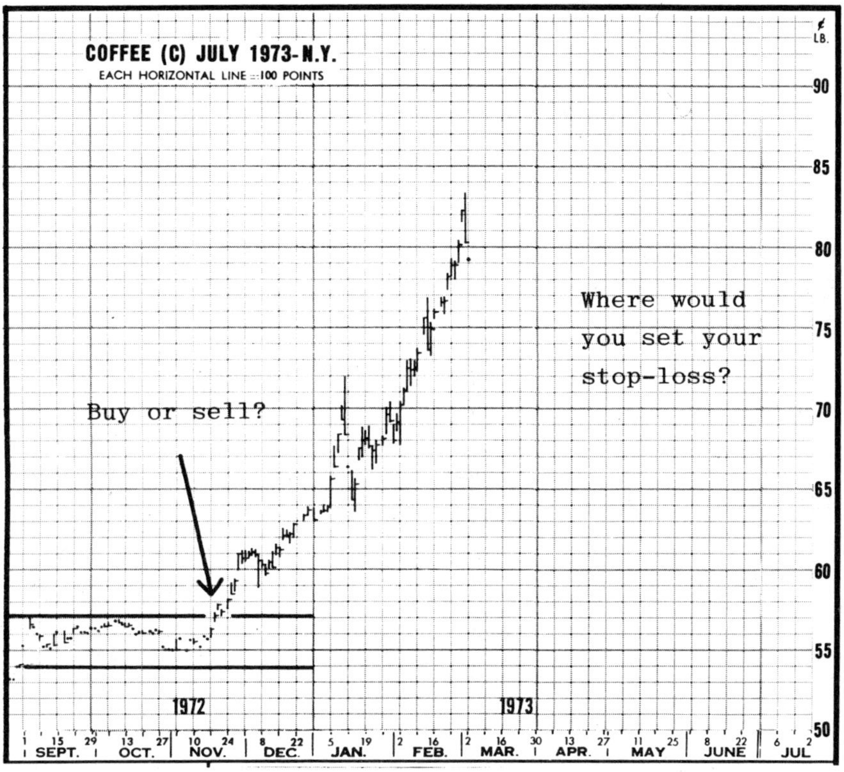

COFFEE: *THE RUN-UP IN COFFEE PRICES BROUGHT THE FUTURES TRADER A 1,950 PERCENT PROFIT, OR $9,750 PER CONTRACT.*

FOREIGN CURRENCIES CAN BE TRADED WITH THE SAME BASIC PRINCIPLES APPLIED TO FUTURES CONTRACTS IN WHEAT, CORN, OR ANY OTHER COMMODITY.

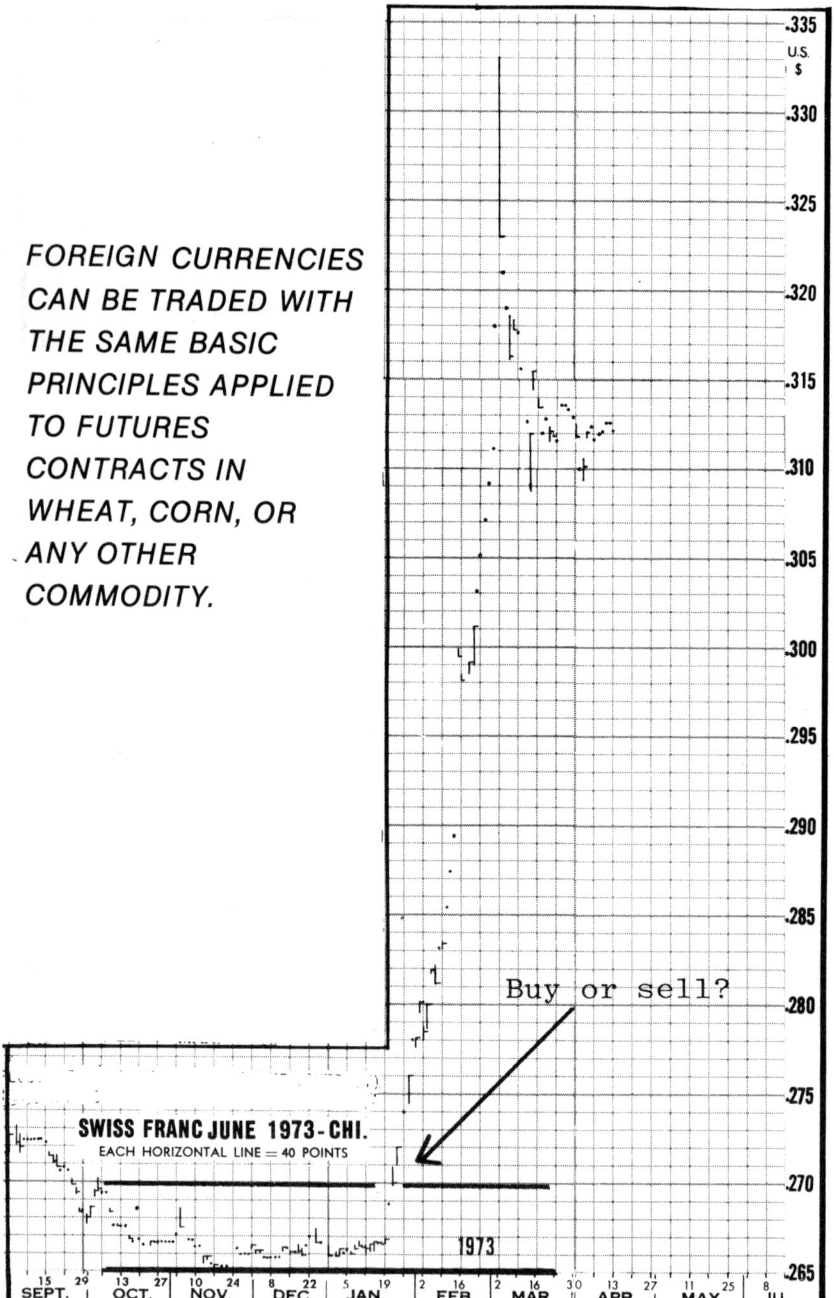

SWISS FRANCS: *POTENTIAL PROFIT IN TWO MONTHS WAS $15,000 PER CONTRACT.*

***BARLEY:** $500 IN DEPOSITED MARGIN MONEY RETURNS $6,250 AS PRICES NEARLY DOUBLE IN A MERE SIX MONTHS.*

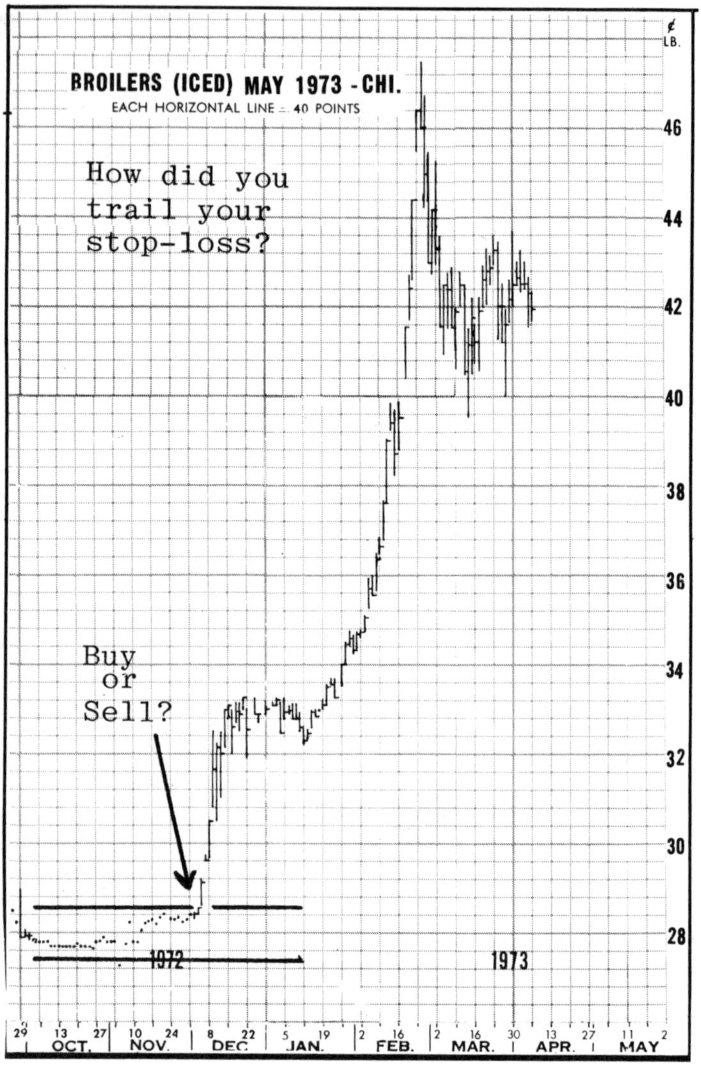

BROILERS: *A MAXIMUM PROFIT OF $4,912 ON A MARGIN OF $400, OR A 1,128 PERCENT RETURN ON INVESTED CAPITAL.*

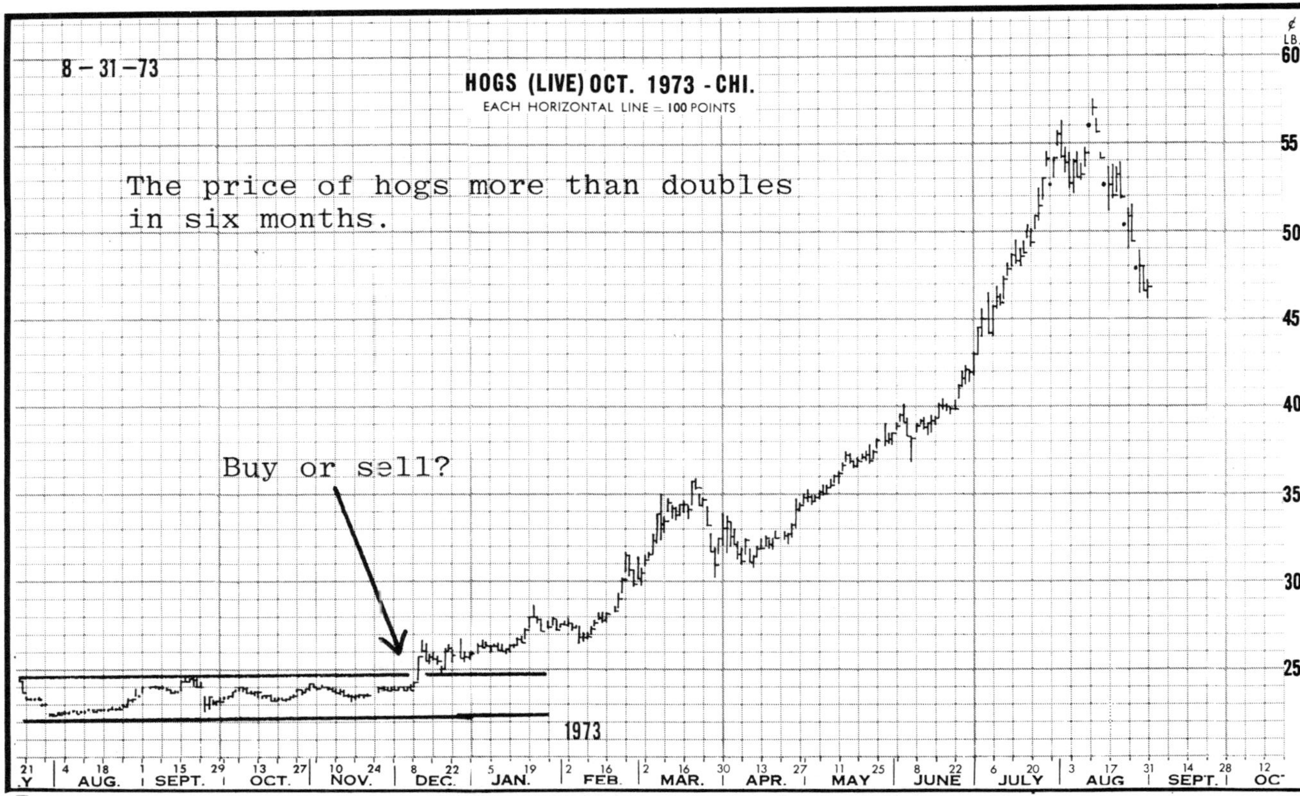

HOGS: *THE 32¢ RISE IN HOG FUTURES MEANT A RETURN OF $9,600 PER CONTRACT, OR 3,200 PERCENT OF ORIGINAL MARGIN.*

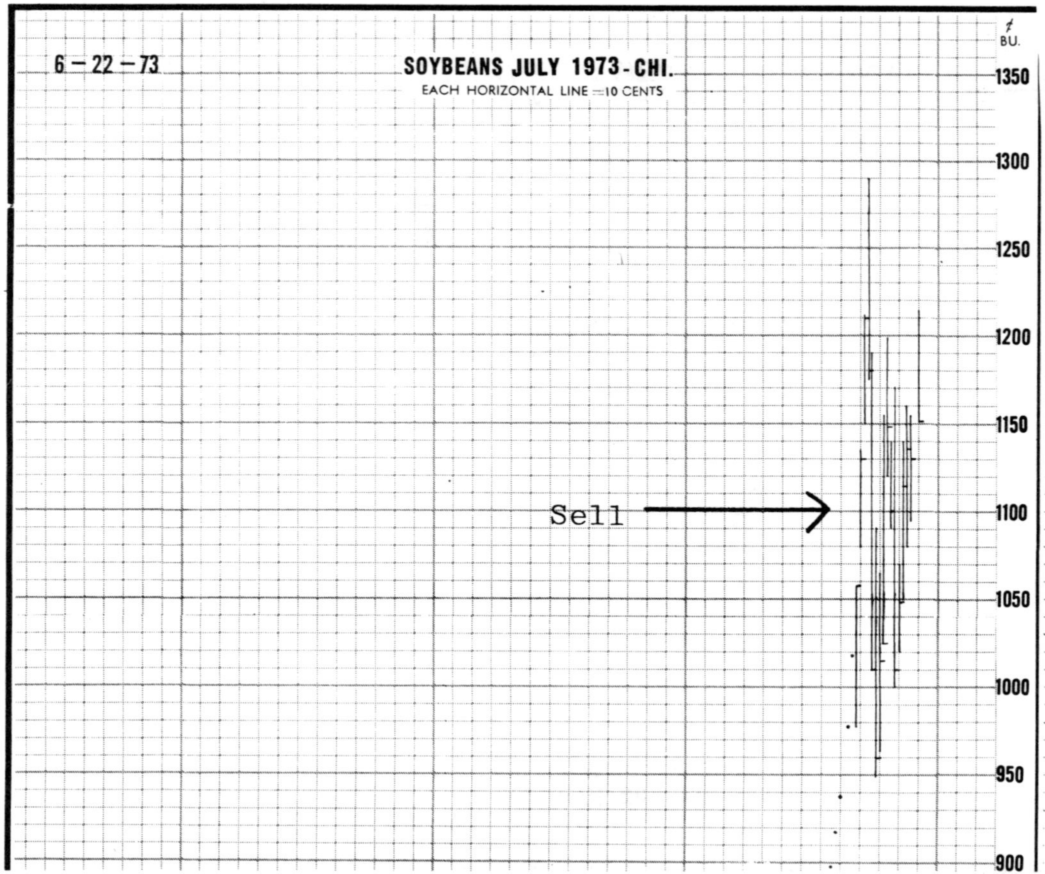

The incredible 1973 bull market in soybeans made headlines around the country. In just eight months, the July futures price soared from $3.50 to almost $13.00!!

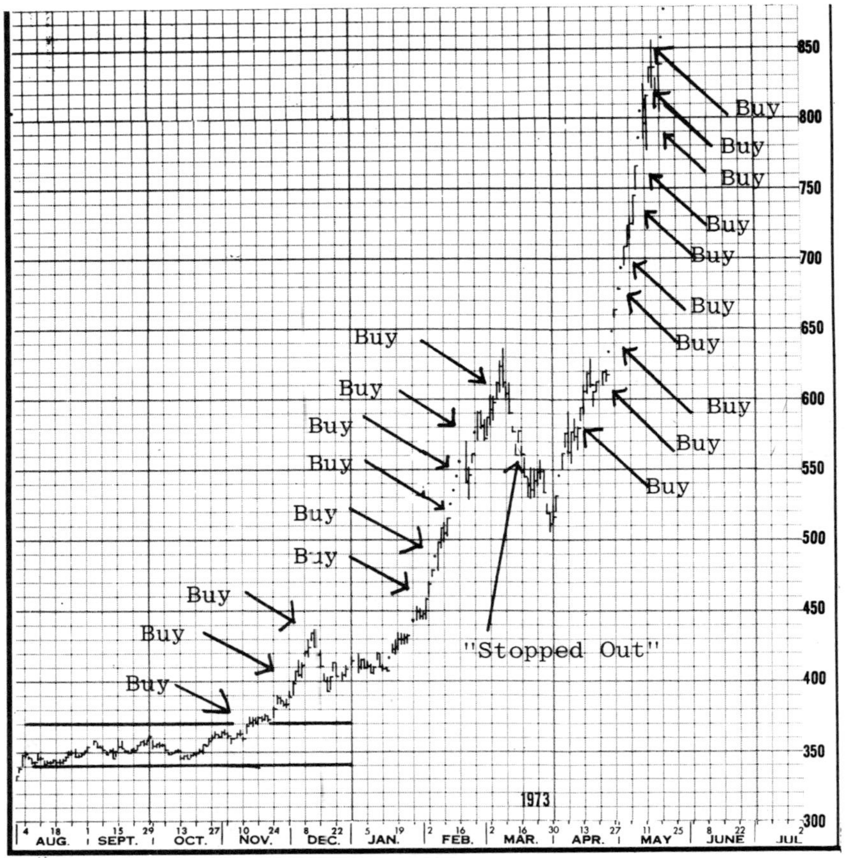

Trading with the method, an average trader could have scaled-in purchases to accumulate enormous profits. Such a series could have typically yielded $224,000 on an original margin of $1000!!

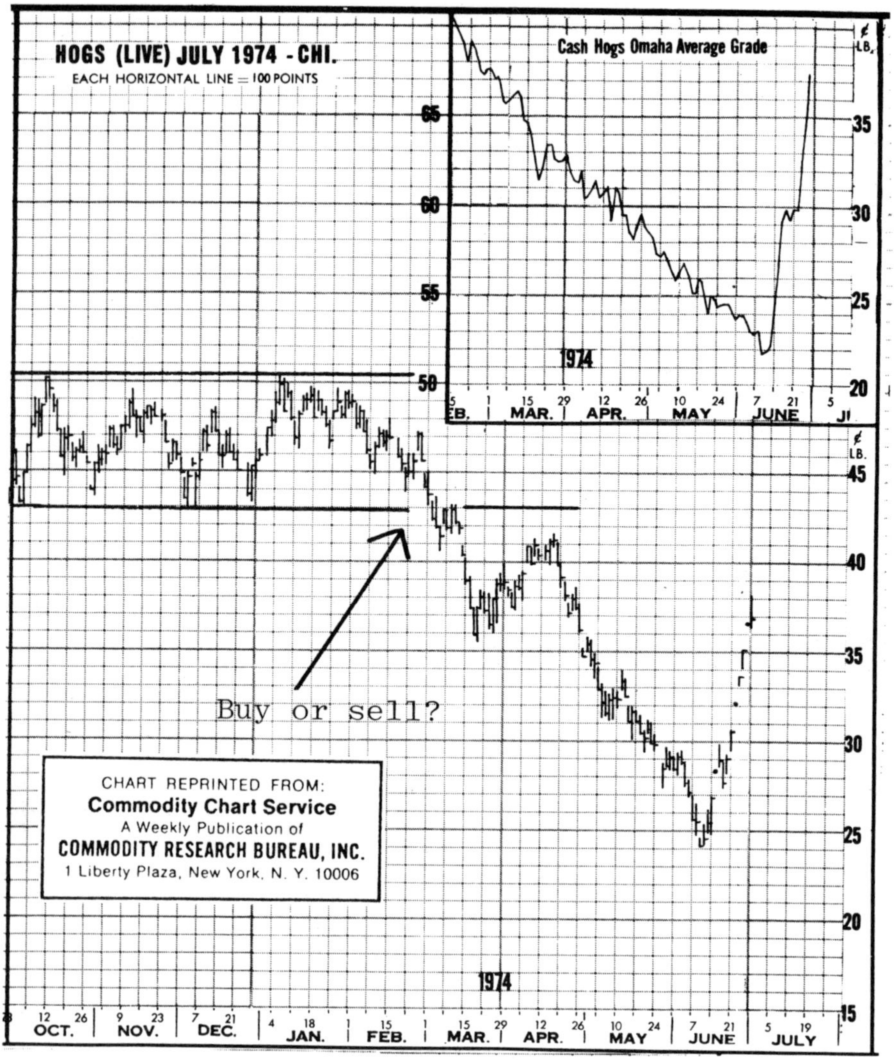

HOG PRICES SUFFER A REVERSAL. PROFITS ON THE SHORT SIDE WERE $5,400 PER CONTRACT, RETURNING 771 PERCENT ON A MARGIN OF $700.

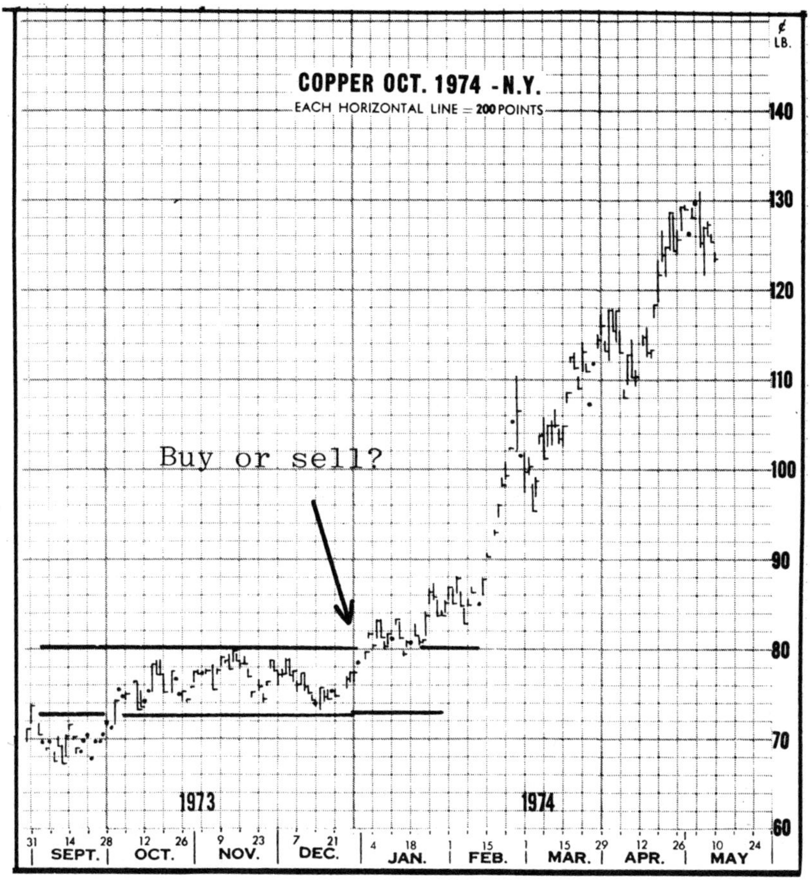

***COPPER:** RISING PRICES BROUGHT A PROFIT OF 1,666 PERCENT ON A MARGIN OF $750, FOR A NET OF $12,500 PER CONTRACT.*

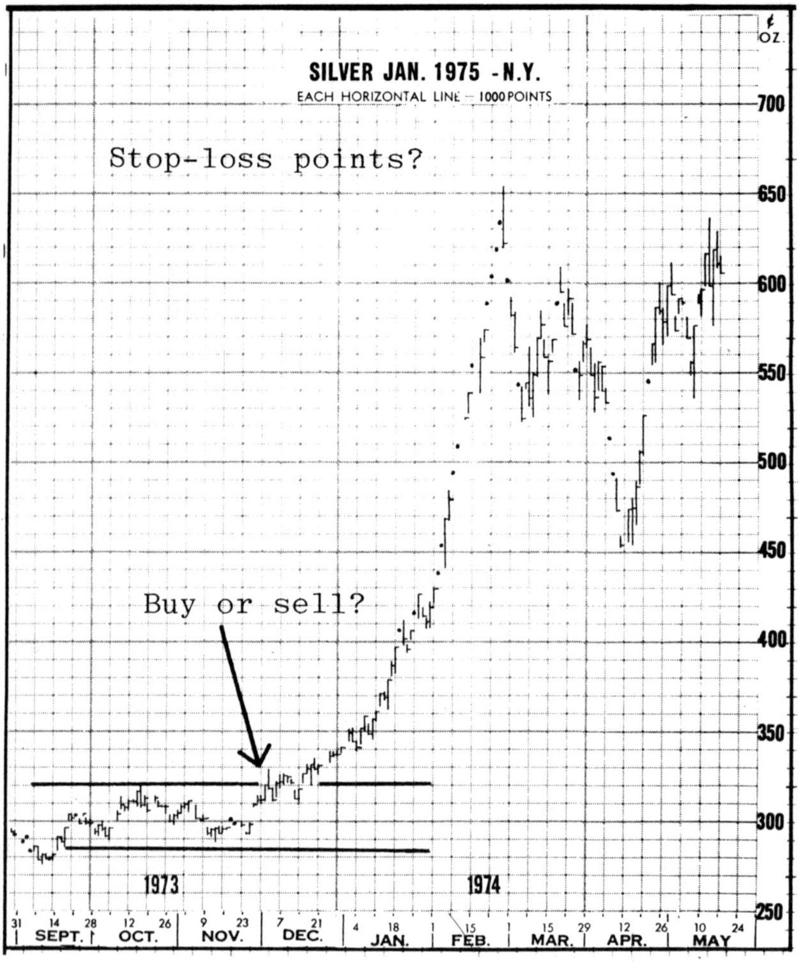

SILVER: *THE ACTION IN THE PRECIOUS METALS WAS WIDESPREAD IN 1974. JANUARY SILVER CONTRACTS BROUGHT PROFITS OF $15,500 PER CONTRACT ON A $1,000 MARGIN.*

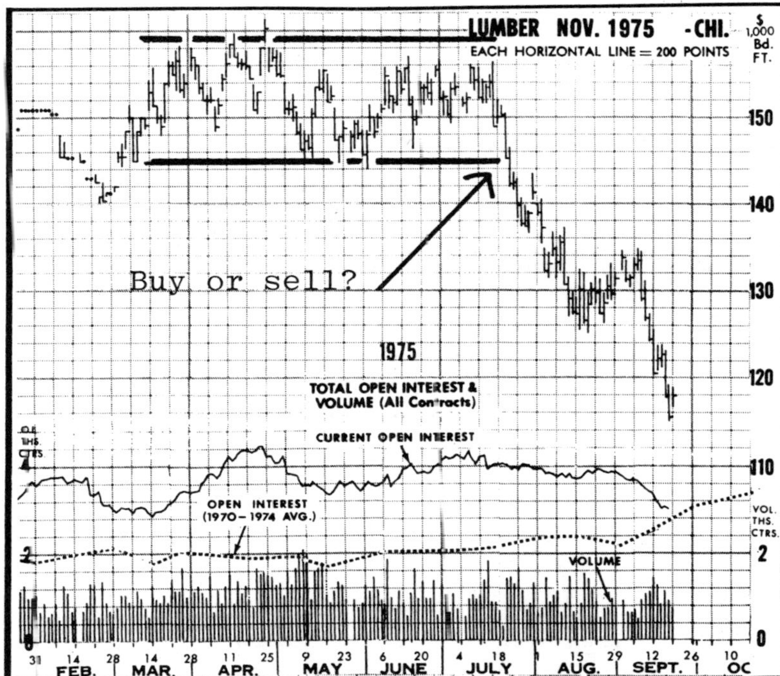

LUMBER: *PROFIT WAS $2,600 PER CONTRACT.*

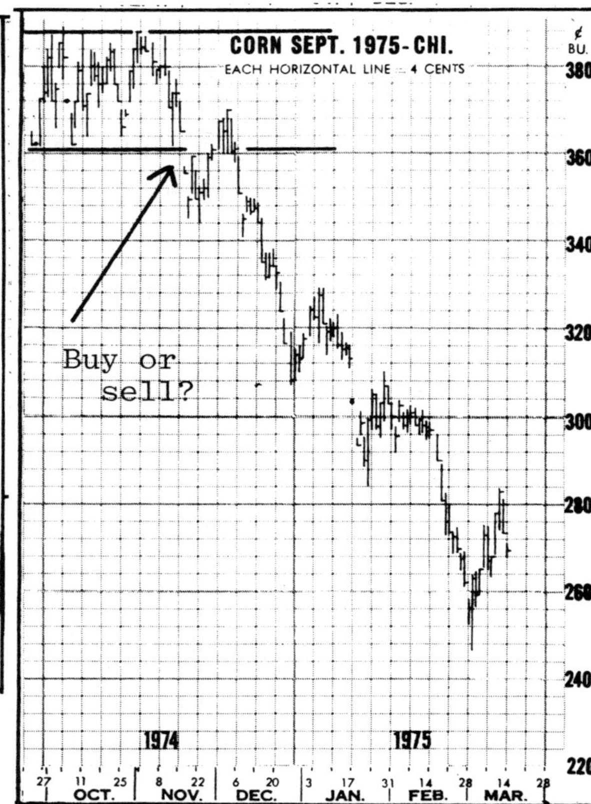

CORN: *PROFIT WAS $4,000 PER CONTRACT.*

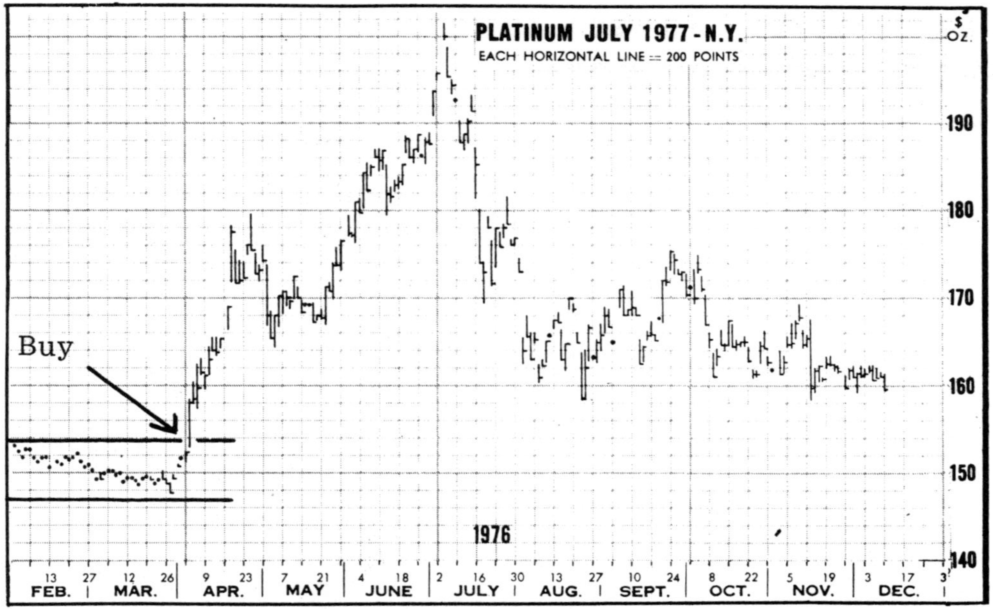

PLATINUM: *IN THE EARLY MONTHS OF 1976, DIFFERENT METALS WENT DIFFERENT WAYS. THE UPWARD BREAKOUT OF PLATINUM WAS WORTH $2,300 PER CONTRACT.*

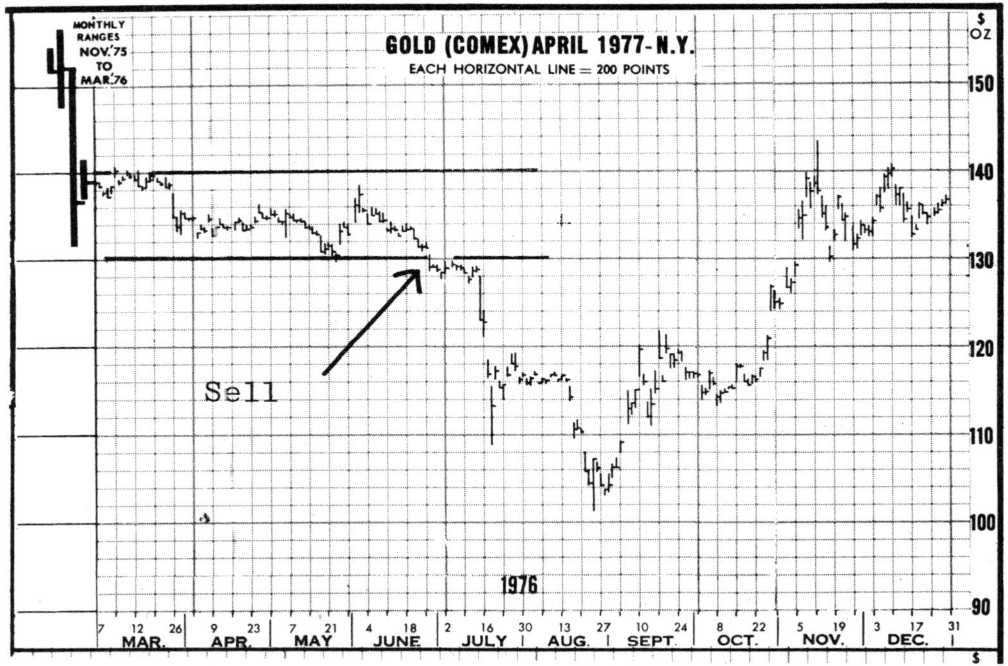

GOLD: *THE DOWN TURN IN GOLD MADE FOR A PROFIT OF $2,900 PER CONTRACT IN LESS THAN TWO MONTHS.*

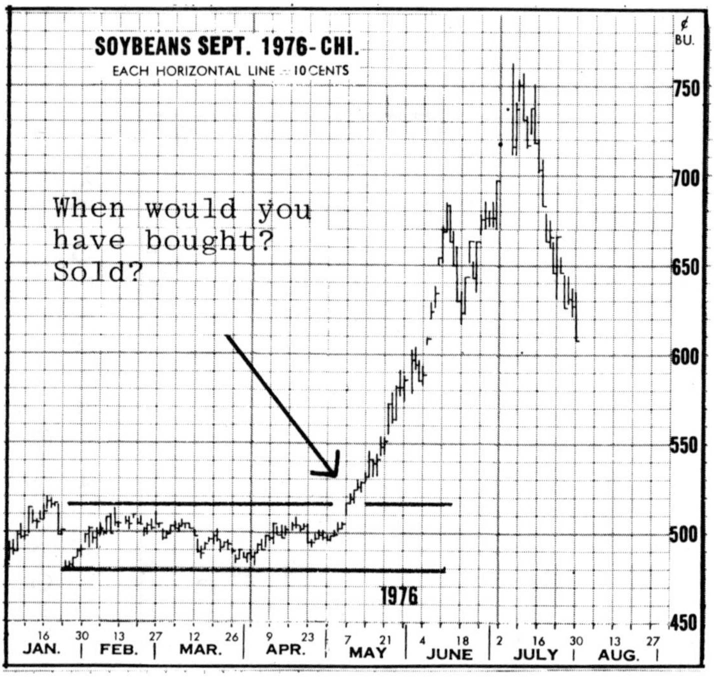

SOYBEANS: *IN 1976, THE SOYBEAN GROUP MOVED TOGETHER. PROFIT IN SOYBEANS AFTER THE BREAKOUT UPWARD FROM THE SIDEWAYS CHANNEL WAS $11,500 PER CONTRACT, ON A MARGIN OF $1,000.*

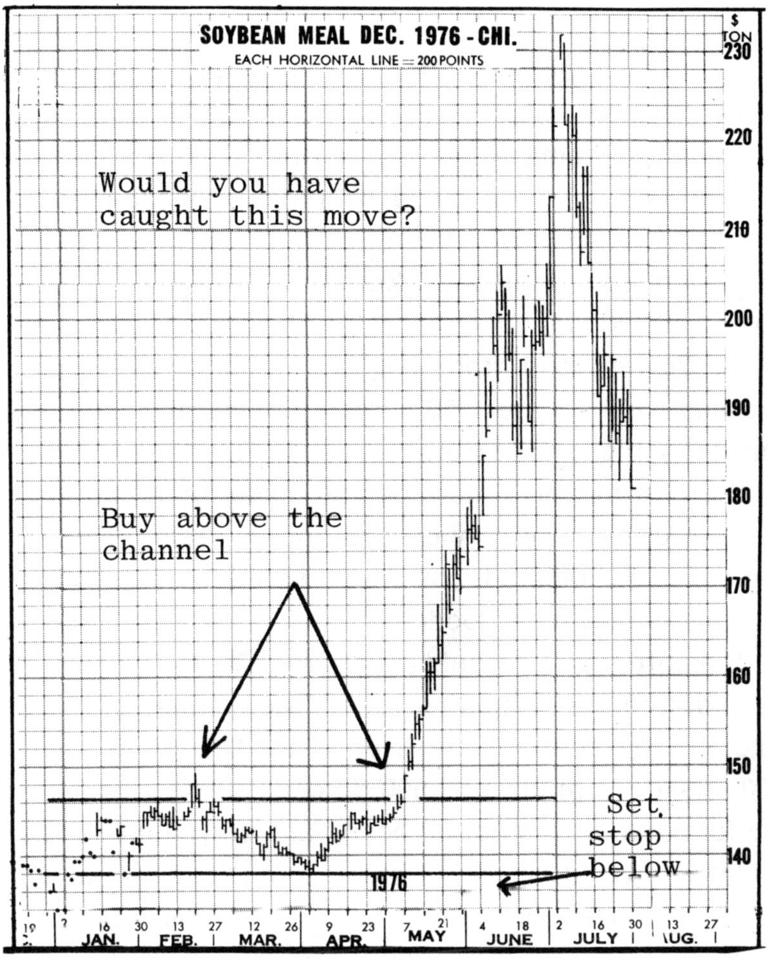

SOYBEAN MEAL: *MEAL PAID $8,400 FOR EACH $1,000 INVESTED.*

COMMENTARY: 1973 through 1976

1973 was a record-shattering year in the history book of futures trading. Seasoned professionals looked on in amazement as commodity after commodity made incredible price moves that have since become legendary. Soybean meal, which had never been higher than $125 a ton in American history, soared to $400 a ton. Wheat advanced to $6 a bushel, it's all time American high. The price of cocoa nearly tripled. Cotton rose from 28¢ a pound to 98¢ a pound. Soybeans went up over 350 percent. In virtually every major commodity, high prices were the rule and not the exception. It was the year in which more people made more money than ever before in the history of commodity trading. If you had been using our method, you would barely have had time to count the money as it flooded in.

The coffee trader would have earned $9,750 on each $500 invested, a return of 1,950 percent. The speculator in Swiss Franc futures contracts realized a $15,000 profit on each $1,000 risked, a return of 1,500 percent in **two months time.** Even for a trader who got on board late, stayed too long, and liquidated well after the reversal, profits, as compared to returns on conventional investments, were staggering.

The stories were much the same in October Hogs, May Broilers and October Barley. It is rare indeed that a general bull (or bear) market occurs in commodity futures. Groups of related commodities may move together, or in reaction to one another, but since each commodity has its own unique supply/demand equation, price fluctuations remain fairly independent. The price of wheat can plummet while gold rises; T-Bills can sink while orange juice skyrockets; pork bellies can slump while potatoes go through the roof. In 1973, however, the majority of commodity markets were pulled upward together by an unusually strong and abnormal set of national and international economic events that exerted an irresistable influence on prices. But you need not have known anything about Soviet grain purchases or freezes in the Brazilian coffee growing regions. The lines on the charts told the tale: narrow trading ranges suddenly penetrated by a breakout. The rest was history, and money in the bank. Profits in October Barley were $6,250 per contract, or 1,250 percent of the $500 margin. The May 1973 Broiler contract (at 28,000 lbs.) paid a maximum of $4,912 on a margin of $400, or 1,228 percent. The 32¢ rise in the price of the October Hogs contract mean a return of $9,600 per contract, or 3,200 percent in nine months.

The performance that topped them all, and that helped put commodities onto the front pages, was that of the once-lowly soybean. How could the average trader have made a fabulous fortune almost automatically in 1973 soybean futures? Let's trace a hypothetical trade by Speculator Smith, an amateur trader of average mental powers who has mastered the method of trading we have been discussing. Prices for the July Soybean contract broke upward through the ceiling of their trading range on November 13, 1972. Having charted soybeans for some months, Smith had a "stop order" to buy at $3.70 resting with the broker, and one contract is bought at this price for a margin of $1000. The stop-loss is set at $3.40.

Prices continue to climb, breaking $4.00, at which point Smith buys another contract. Encouraged as the advance goes on, Smith now sets about establishing a game plan for the big move — a plan of "scaling-in" further purchases every time the price advances another 30 cents. Stop-loss is trailed 50 cents behind the last contract purchased, enough to protect profits and respect a volatile market. By the time prices pass $6.10, Smith controls 9 contracts on the initial margin of $1000 (subsequent contracts having been margined with "paper profits"). A sudden reversal hits, and Smith is stopped out in March at $5.60. Profit on the 9 contracts (7 winners and 2 losers) is $31,500 or 3,150 percent.

But Smith hasn't lost interest in soybeans. Another stop-order to buy is placed at $5.80, above the old stop-loss, just in case the reversal was temporary and the advance unfinished. Smith is back in play by early April, buying contracts every 30¢ and trailing the stop-loss 50¢ behind. The last contract acquired is at $8.50, for from then on "limit" moves and extreme volatility prevent further purchases. Early in June, with the delivery month approaching and prices still gyrating madly, Smith decides to take the money and run. By now, on this second trade, Smith controls 10 soybean futures contracts. All 10 are winners when Smith sells out at $11.00. Profit on this batch of contracts is an astronomical $192,500, or 19,250 percent of the original $1000. Total profits in July 1973 Soybeans: $224,000 (in 1973 dollars!)!!!

In 1974, we had a variety of reactions to the bull market of '73. Hog prices, which peaked during the summer of '73, settled down into a narrow trading range until February of 1974. Support for high prices eventually collapsed under the pressures of adequate supply and reduced demand. Prices head downward, making it possible for the speculator who went long profitably in hogs in 1973 to make another fortune by shorting hogs in 1974, both trades almost effortlessly accomplished by adherence to the method. Profit: $5,400 per contract in July 1974 Hogs, returning 771 percent on a margin of $700.

Copper rose in 1973 from around 50 cents a pound to near the 80 cent level. Futures prices then stabilized in a sideways pattern until the market made up its mind. The bull market here, unlike in hogs, was just beginning. Early in 1974 copper futures resumed the move up, reaching $1.30 by late April. The profit which could have been earned on each $750 invested was $12,500, or $1,666 percent in four months. In a parallel fashion (as often happens in a related group of commodities such as the precious metals), silver continued the move that took the average futures price in 1973 from $2.00 to $3.00 an ounce. After calming for some months, the January 1975 contract took off at the start of 1974. Here profits were $15,500 per contract on a margin investment of only $1,000.

Lumber and corn were among the winners in 1975. Corn prices too had been swept up in the madness of '73 when the average monthly cash price of corn nearly doubled. Prices then fell back sharply, but soared once more in 1974 to record highs. Those highs became the channel range you see depicted on the chart for September 1975 Corn. Corn repeated its tendency to retrace big gains, and in doing so brought traders hefty sums, about $4,000 on each $700 margin.

Lumber was also a quite volatile commodity during this period. It had made high peaks and deep lows in both 1973 and 1974, riding the roller coaster that took many commodities and traders for a ride. Such volatility is difficult to trade, and dangerous, unless patterns that are tradeable develop. Otherwise the careless speculator is wiped out by wildly fluctuating price moves. But the November 1975 Lumber contract presented an attractive opportunity. Here you could have discovered a pattern in the wild career of lumber prices. After so many ups and downs, the speculator who learns from history comes to expect the formation of narrow trading ranges in the wake of severe price volatility. Prices in such periods are said to be "consolidating," as the market reevaluates conditions before continuing the previous big move or reversing direction. The November contract fits the model, and returns $2,600 per contract on a margin of $600 to the trader who has been accurately monitoring the action.

An interesting turn of events brought traders in precious metals considerable rewards in 1976. Both the April 1977 Gold contract and the July 1977 Platinum contract began the year in steady sideways patterns. Early in April, a speculative run-up in platinum futures began. Gold did nothing. This time the metals group did not move together. The speculator learns another history lesson: general price tendencies or characteristics, like that of the metals to move together, are no substitute for the laws of real price moves. The trader must go where the market goes, no matter how unreasonable the move may seem. Trader Jones, believing that metals just **have** to stick together, might have bought gold ruinously or entirely missed the move in platinum. Trader Smith, who charts real prices, and trades only when the move out of an established range actually begins, gets on the right side of both platinum and gold to profit happily.

The **upward** move in platinum was worth $2,300 per contract. Meanwhile, gold began its **descent** out of its own channel. What happened? The speculator should recall that each commodity, even in a related group, has its own set of fundamentals. Platinum has a unique set of industrial uses, most notably in the catalytic converters used to control automobile pollution. The run-up in platinum may have been sparked by the beginning of serious government pressure to increase fuel economy. Heavy demand for cash platinum, however, did not and could not appear overnight, and supplies remained ample despite a drastic cutback in U.S. production. Prices fell back. The chart trader, again, need have known none of this to have reaped the balance of the available profits in the move.

Gold, which had hit new highs in 1973 and 1974, started to decline in early 1975. The first months of 1976 were a consolidation period. Perhaps fueled by the disappointing collapse in the platinum market, gold decided to resume its downward move in July to test the bottom. You stood to make a maximum of $2,900 per contract in two months. After all this uncertainty, gold and platinum both ended the year right back where they started.

Our old friends soybean and soybean meal were, that very same year, demonstrating how related commodities **can** move in harmony. Profits in soybeans: $11,500 for each $1,000 invested. Profits in soybean meal: $8,400 for each $1,000 risked.

* * * * * * * * * * * * * * * * *

These case histories document the excitement of futures tradng today. Year after year, new contracts begin to form those little lines on the charts that mean riches for the skillful trader. As you practice analyzing the charts and playing the markets, let yourself feel the challenge and thrill that come with successful speculation. The rewards of futures trading are personal as well as economic. Managing your own account, evaluating the markets with your own skills, making decisions based on your own expertise, you will come to know yourself better. There is an exhilaration in knowing that **you** are responsible for your own success, that **you** have the talent and knowledge to make the market deliver.

For a final review, examine the following graphs from the years 1977 through 1980. These were boom years in futures trading, when thousands of new speculators entered the markets. **The vast majority of these people lost money!** Knowing what you now know about trading commodity futures, would **you** have been a loser in those years? Or would you have been one of the successful traders who caught the big moves and took home the big profits?

CORN: *PRICE BREAKS THROUGH THE FLOOR OF A LONG ESTABLISHED CHANNEL. PROFITS ON THE SHORT SIDE WERE $5,400 PER CONTRACT.*

COCOA: *COCOA PRICES TRIPLED IN A YEAR. CALCULATE HOW YOU COULD HAVE EARNED OVER $1 MILLION ON A $2,000 INVESTMENT. MARGIN WAS $1,000 PER CONTRACT. EVERY 1¢ MOVE WAS WORTH $300.*

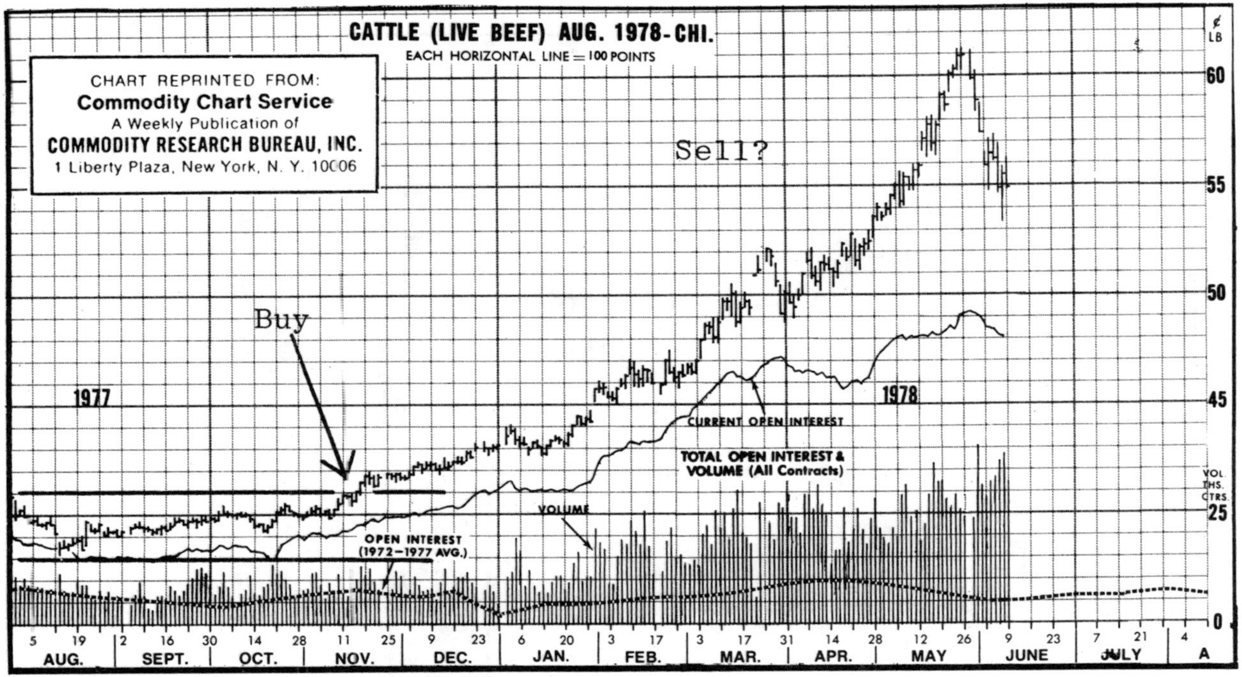

CATTLE: *THE UPWARD BREAKOUT IN CATTLE SENT PRICES FROM 41¢ TO 61¢ IN SIX MONTHS. POTENTIAL PROFIT TO THE TRADER: $8,000 PER CONTRACT.*

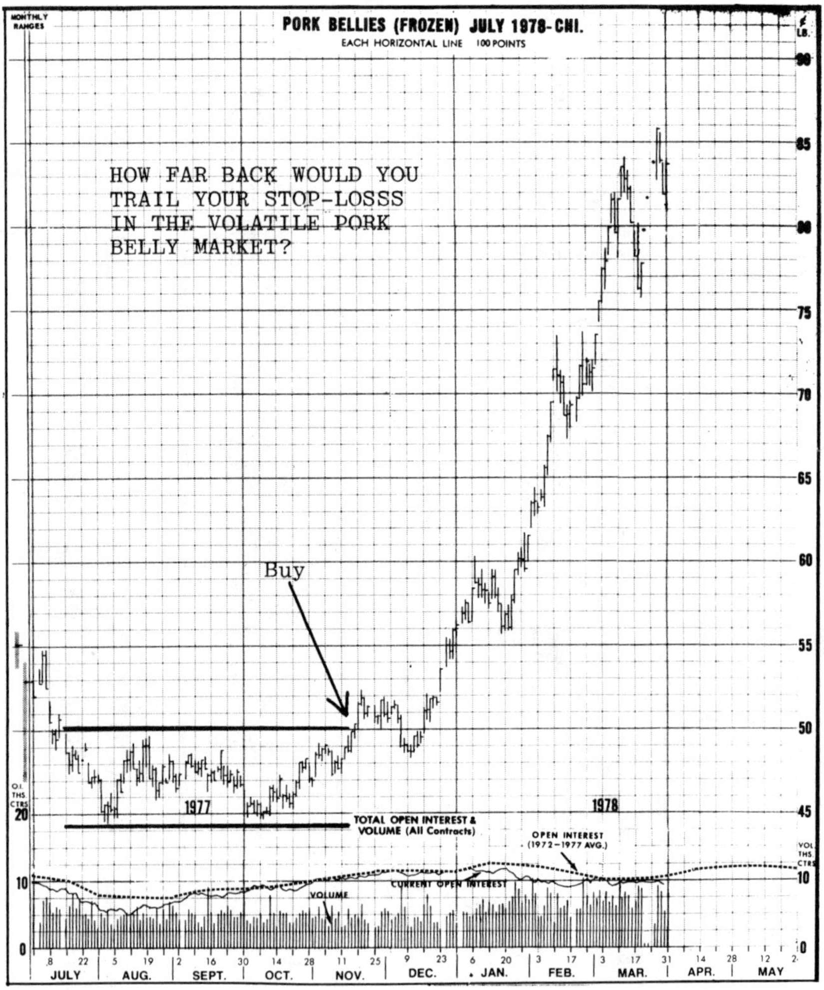

PORK BELLIES: *PROFITS ON THE LONG SIDE WERE $12,600 PER CONTRACT.*

WHEAT: *PROFITS ON THE DECEMBER CONTRACT AT CHICAGO WERE $8,250.*

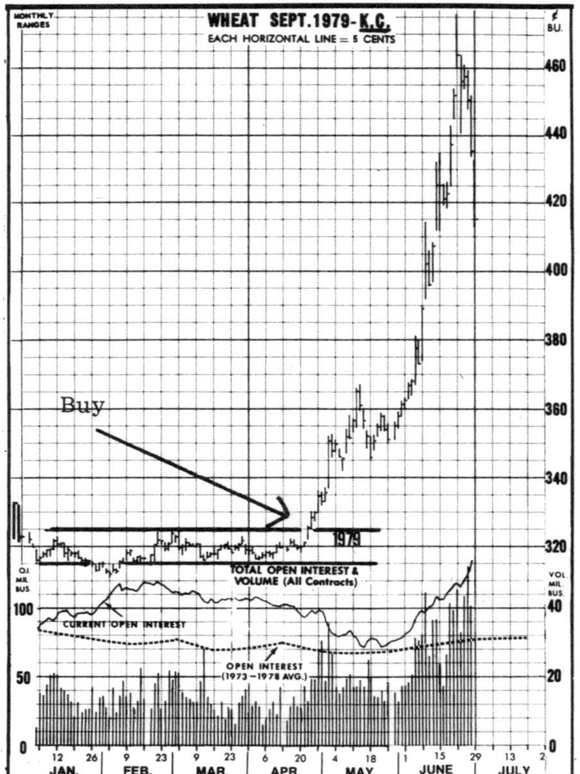

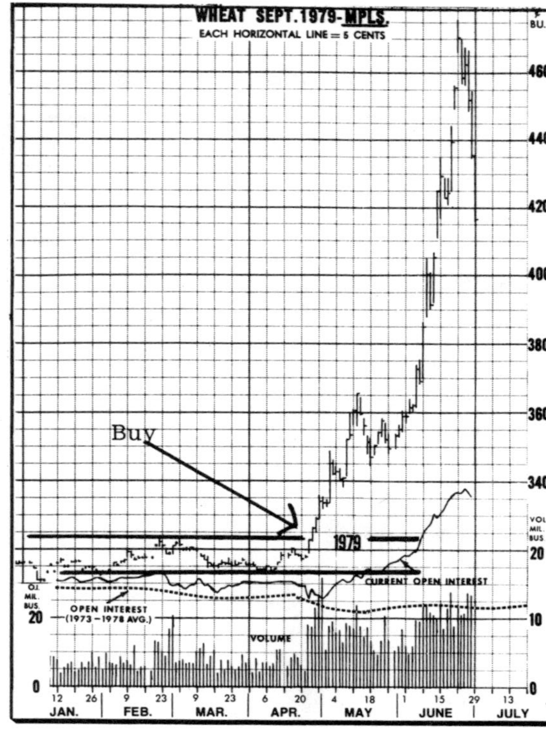

THE MOVE IN WHEAT INCLUDES CONTRACTS AT KANSAS CITY AND MINNEAPOLIS. PROFIT ON EACH WAS $7,500 PER CONTRACT.

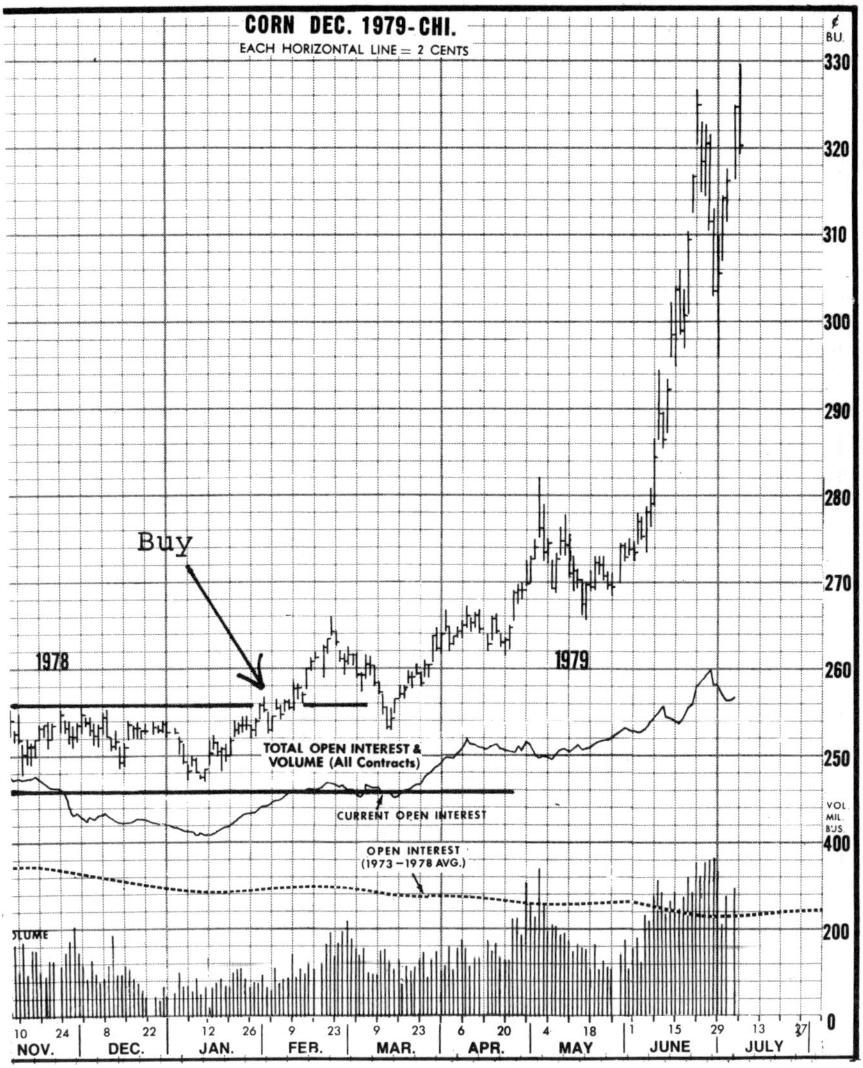

***CORN:** THE PATTERN IS REPEATED. PROFIT WAS $3,500 PER CONTRACT ON A MARGIN OF $600.*

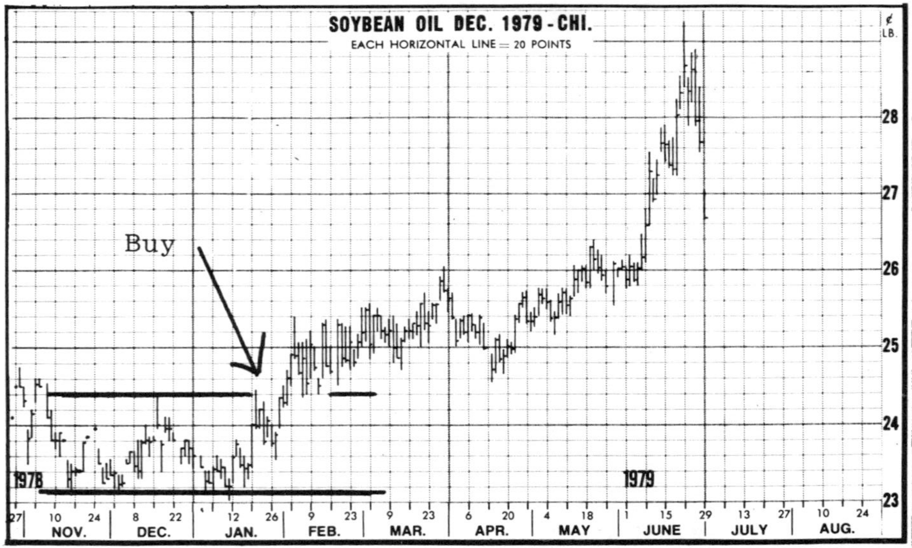

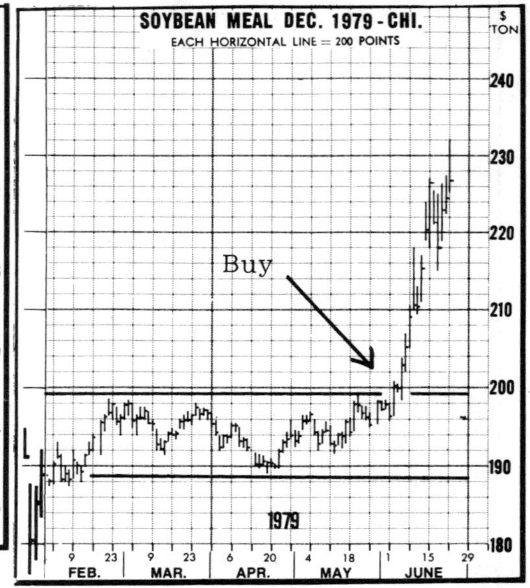

SOYBEAN OIL AND SOYBEAN MEAL: *THE PATTERN EXTENDS TO THE SOY COMPLEX FOR 1979. PROFITS IN OIL: $2,880 PER CONTRACT; PROFITS IN MEAL: $3,000.*

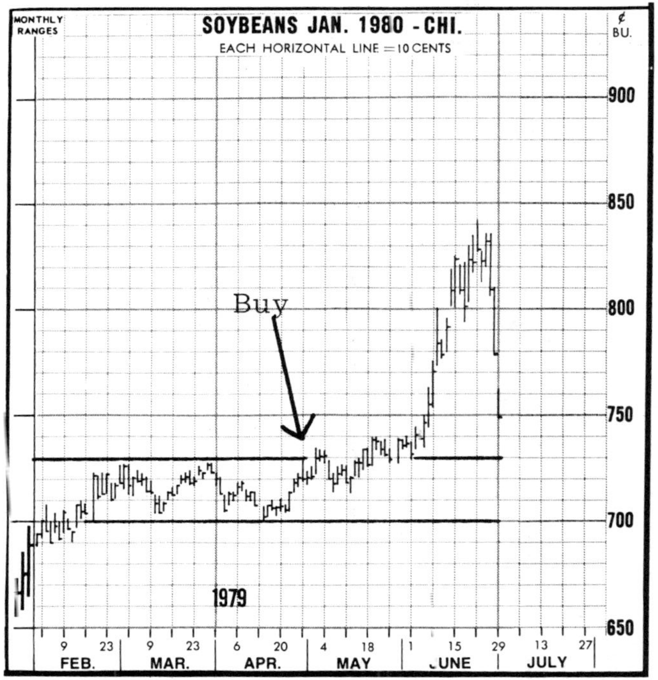

SOYBEANS: *BEANS BROUGHT A PROFIT OF $5,500 PER CONTRACT ON $1,200 MARGIN.*

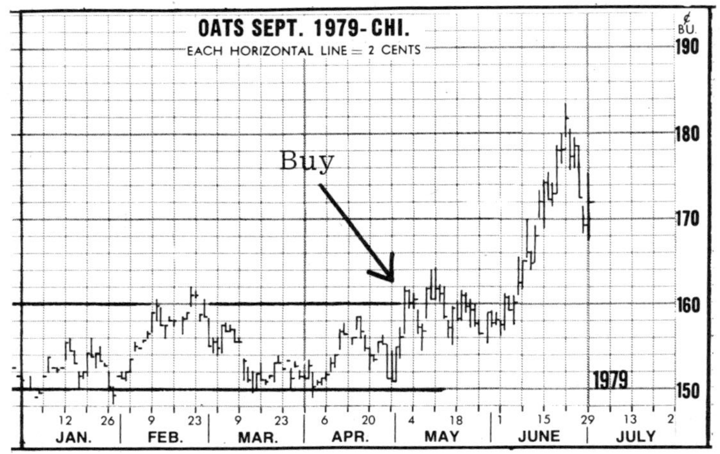

OATS: *$1,200 PROFIT ON A MARGIN OF $500.*

GOLD: *THE PRECIOUS METALS WENT WILD IN 1979-1980. PROFIT ON THE OCTOBER CONTRACT WAS $40,000.*

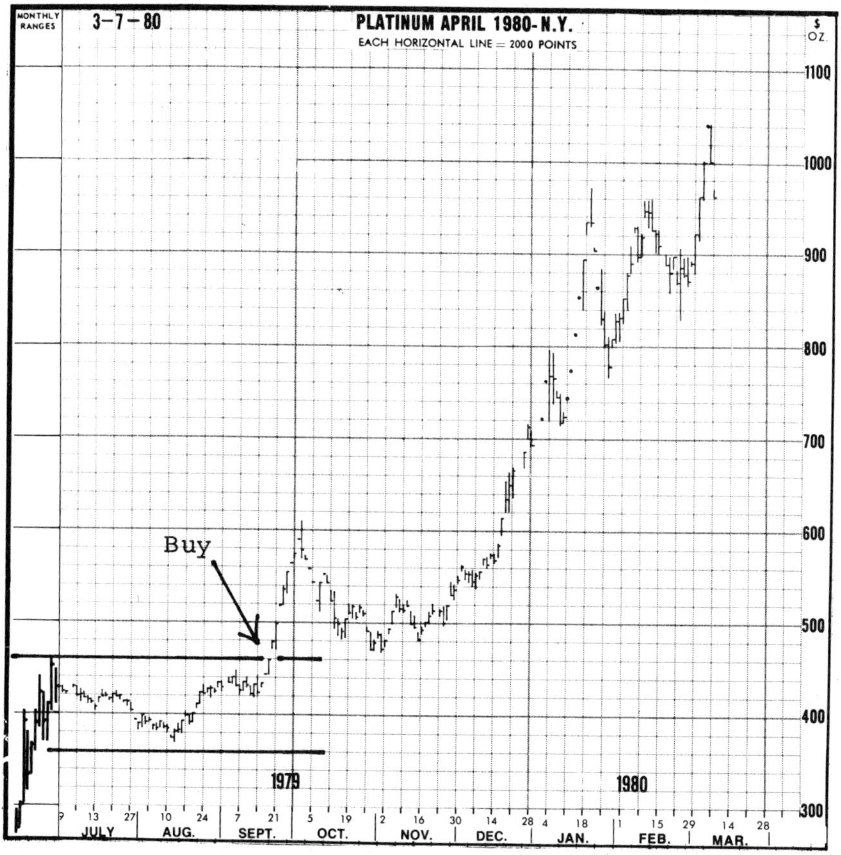

***PLATINUM:** COMPARE THIS BREAKOUT WITH THE CHARTS FOR GOLD AND SILVER. PROFIT PER CONTRACT WAS $22,500.*

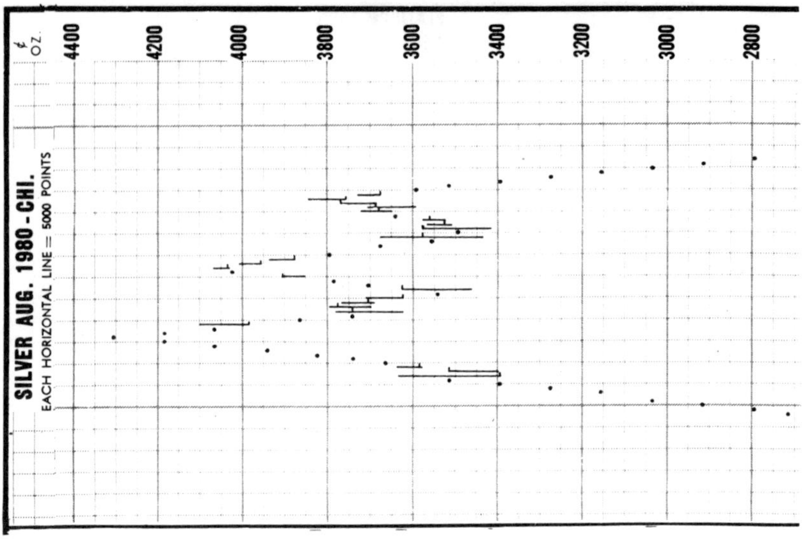

SILVER: *A NOW LEGENDARY BOOM AND BUST THAT SENT SHOCK WAVES THROUGH THE FUTURES INDUSTRY. AN AVERAGE TRADER USING OUR METHOD COULD HAVE REALIZED A PROFIT OF $137,000 PER CONTRACT ON A MARGIN OF $1,000!!*

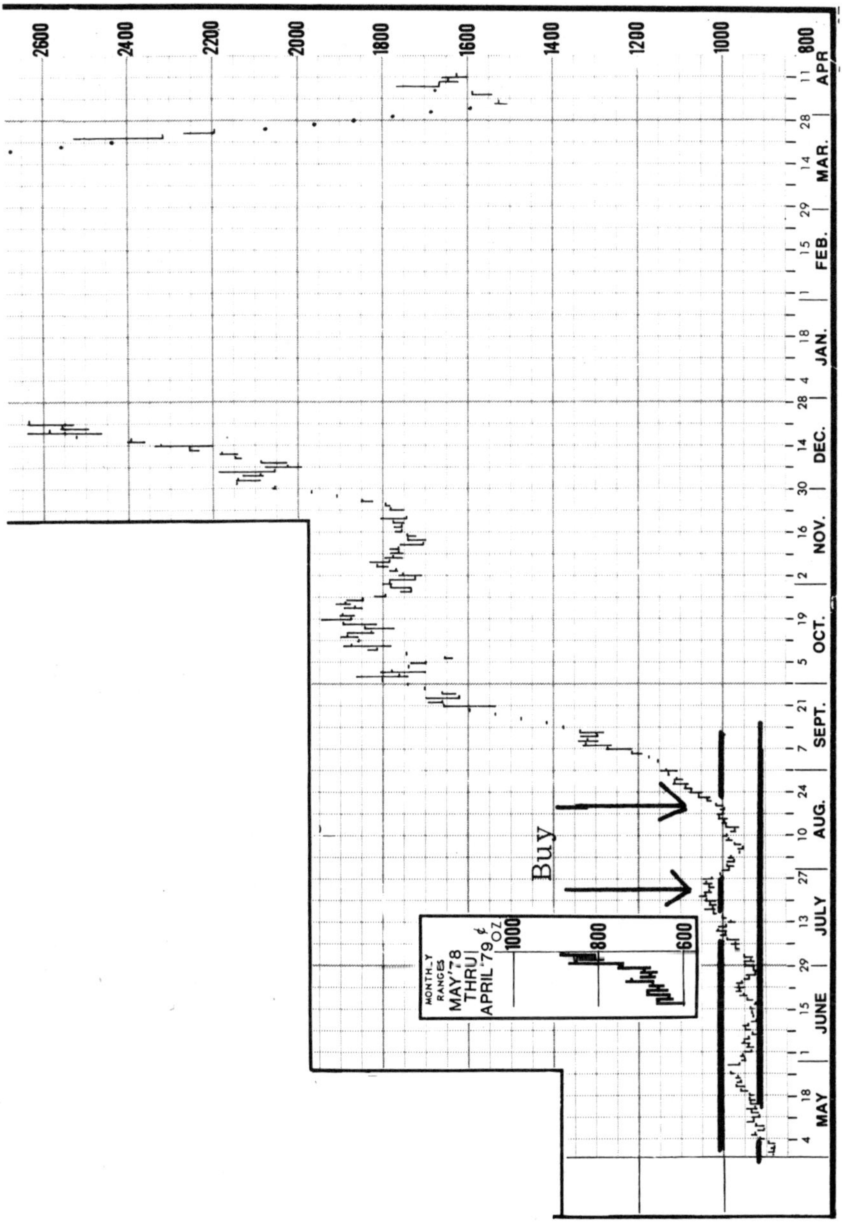
2600
2400
2200
2000
1800
1600
1400
1200
1000
800
MAY
JUNE
JULY
AUG.
SEPT.
OCT.
NOV.
DEC.
JAN.
FEB.
MAR.
APR.
Buy
MONTHLY RANGES
MAY '78
THRU
APRIL '79
¢ OZ
1000
800
600

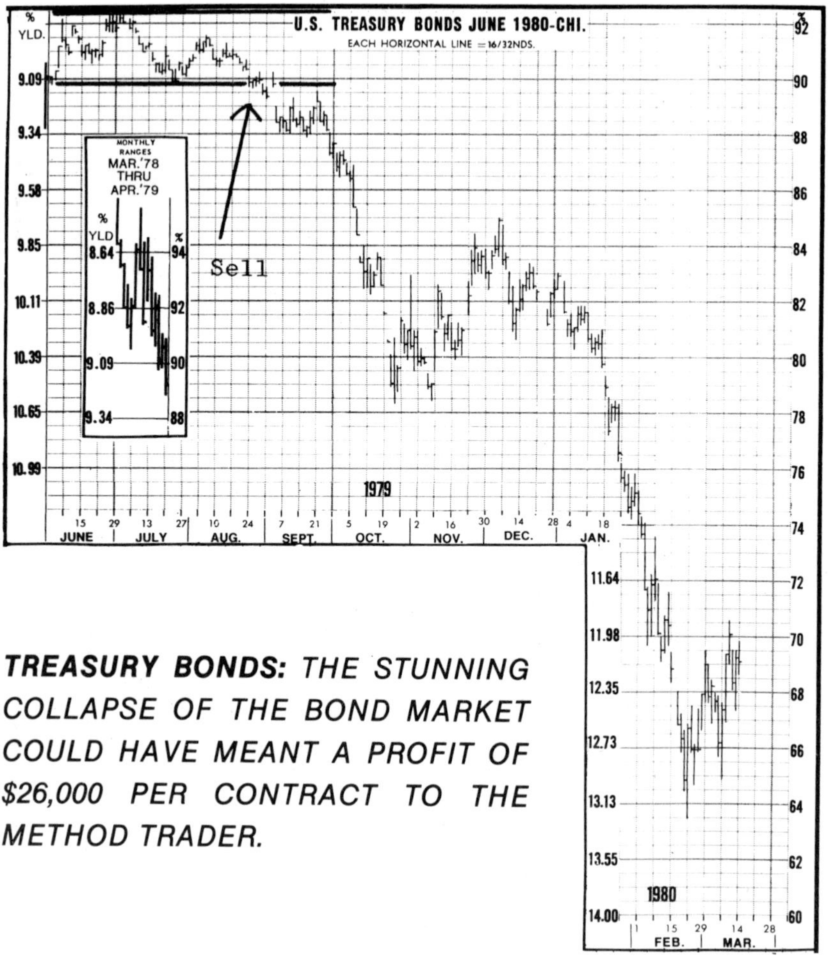

TREASURY BONDS: *THE STUNNING COLLAPSE OF THE BOND MARKET COULD HAVE MEANT A PROFIT OF $26,000 PER CONTRACT TO THE METHOD TRADER.*

SUGAR: AFTER EIGHT MONTHS OF SMALL PRICE FLUCTUATIONS IN A SIDEWAYS CHANNEL, THE UPWARD BREAKOUT FINALLY COMES. SUGAR PRICES DOUBLE, AND THE TRADER REALIZES A PROFIT OF $30,240 PER CONTRACT ON A $3,000 MARGIN.

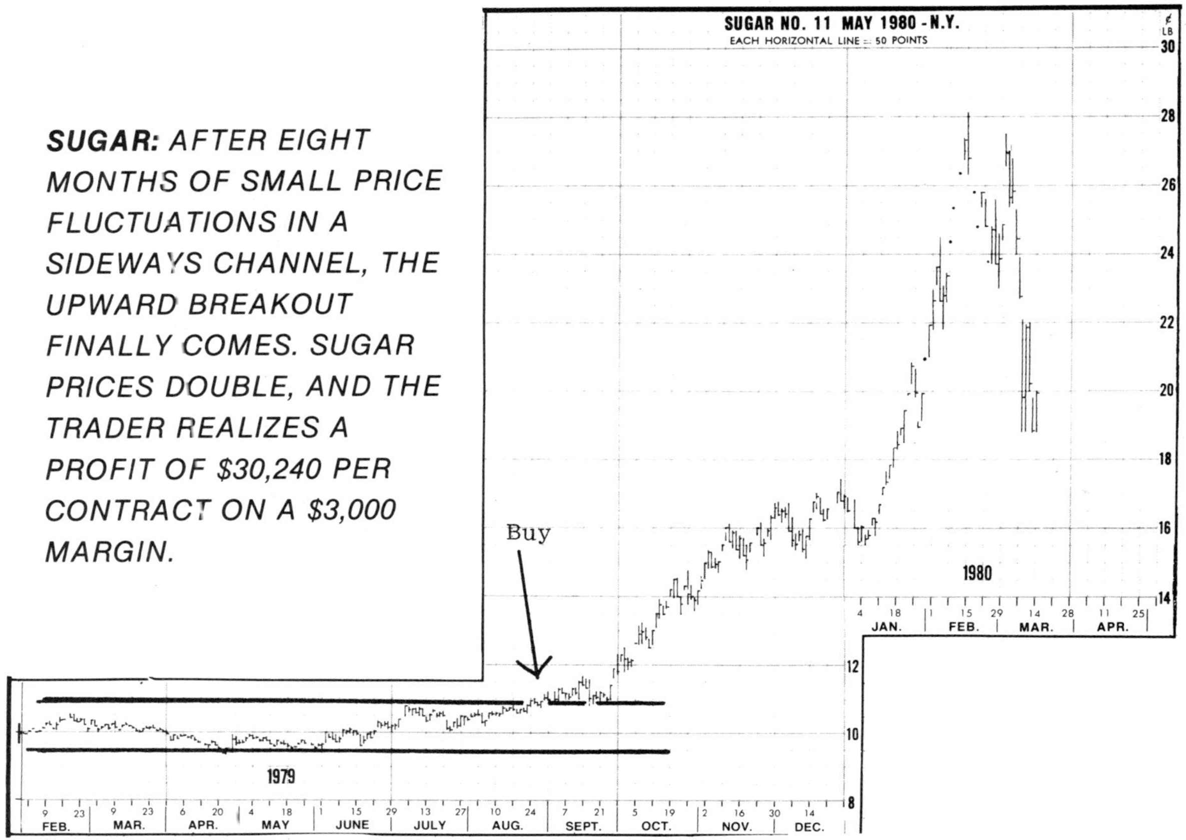

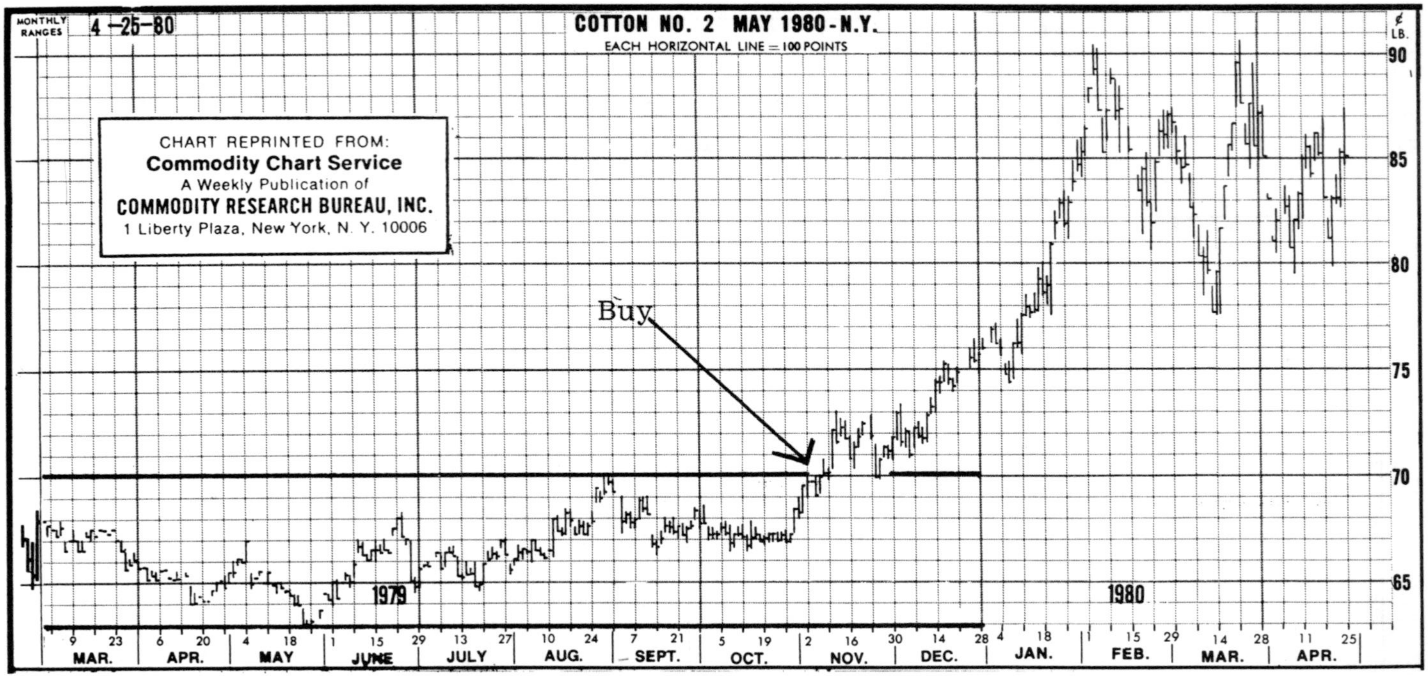

COTTON: *THIS BULL MARKET WAS WORTH $10,000 PER CONTRACT ON A MARGIN OF $1,000.*

COMMENTARY: 1977 through 1980

When we last looked at corn, back in 1975, distant futures prices had fallen back to a range between $2.50 and $2.80. In 1976, futures prices edged sideways, then abruptly hit a high near $3.20 before descending even further than the lows of 1975. In 1977, corn once more traded in a close range as the year began. This time, however, things were different. 1973 and 1974 had been years of successive record-high prices, and correspondingly sharp collapses. In 1975, the high was again a sharp peak, but it failed to reach anywhere near the high set in 1974. In 1976, once again the year's high, though distinguished, fell short of the high for the previous year. And the years' lows were getting successively lower. In 1977, the bottom dropped out of the corn futures markets. It was the final downtrend correction to the great highs of '73 and '74. The reasons for the obvious chart cycles could be found in supply and demand. World corn production had actually declined in 1972 and 1974, while demand, spurred by growth in population and in livestock requiring feed, increased. After dipping in 1974, U.S. corn production rose steadily, encouraged by the high prices and strong markets. World production also rose. Inevitably, these successive record harvests chipped away at corn prices, year after year, until the abundance brought prices in August of 1977 to a four-year low. Profits per contract on a short sale were $5,400.

The speculator who was exhausted by all this action in the grain markets might have turned to the cocoa futures contract for an easy ride. Like sugar and coffee, cocoa is a world commodity subject to extreme price fluctuations in response to a very erratic supply and demand equation. In 1976-77 world cocoa bean production hit a nine-year low. Harvests in 1975-76 had trailed the record crop of the year before. The result: cocoa futures in 1977 hit a price **7 times** higher than the average price in 1970. At a profit of $300 for every 1 cent move in the price of cocoa, figure for yourself when you could have gotten into the market, and what your profits would have been. You could conceivably have retired on this trade alone.

(How? Let's say you bought two contracts when prices broke the old ceiling at 60¢, with a margin deposit of $1000 per contract. You continue to scale-in your purchases, buying two contracts each time that prices rise another 4¢, financing the trades with profits on the earlier contracts. Stop-loss is trailed 20¢ behind. After buying 72 contracts, you would have been stopped out at the reversal to $1.80. All 60 contracts bought at prices below $1.80 bring profits, while the ten purchased above $1.80 cause no gain or loss. Total profits on your $2000 investment: **$1,083,600 or 54,180 percent.**)

1978 was a banner year for method traders following the markets in livestock futures. Live cattle prices had hit their last big highs in 1975. Afterward each subsequent year's high was successively lower, dragging down monthly average prices. The lows for the year, however, stabilized in 1977, and prices levelled out into the channel we see forming in mid-1977. This was the time to keep charts up-dated daily and watch for signs of recovery in cattle prices. The breakout up began in November of 1977, and carried the price of the August Live Cattle futures contract to a level of 61 cents a pound by May of 1978. Profit per contract: $8,000.

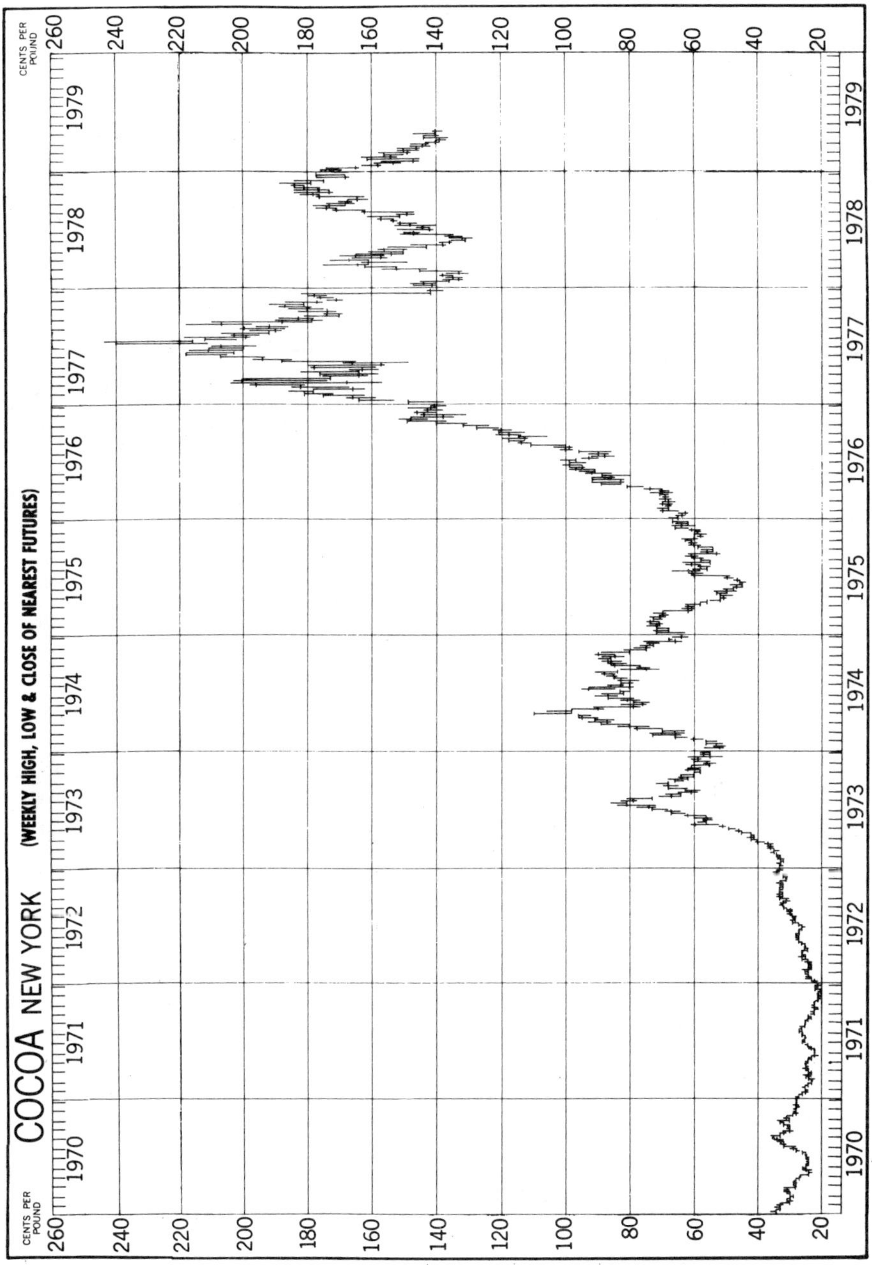
COCOA NEW YORK
(WEEKLY HIGH, LOW & CLOSE OF NEAREST FUTURES)
CENTS PER POUND
260
240
220
200
180
160
140
120
100
80
60
40
20
1970
1971
1972
1973
1974
1975
1976
1977
1978
1979

Even more impressive in 1978 was the action in pork bellies. A virtually parallel recovery to that in cattle futures almost doubled the price of the July 1978 Pork Belly contract. Here, too, prices had hit their record highs in 1975 by going over the $1.00 a pound mark. Once again, highs and lows for 1976 and 1977 showed pork belly prices retracing the big gain of 1975. But the low in 1977 resisted falling below the 45 cent a pound level, and pork belly traders kept their charts handy and looked for a strengthening, or collapse, in prices. The sideways channel in July 1978 Bellies formed in mid-1977 and lasted almost six months. The method trader waited patiently. Once prices made their break, the ascent was steep. In just three months, prices went from 50 cents a pound to 85 cents. On one (old size) contract of 36,000 pounds, profit was a very smart $12,600.

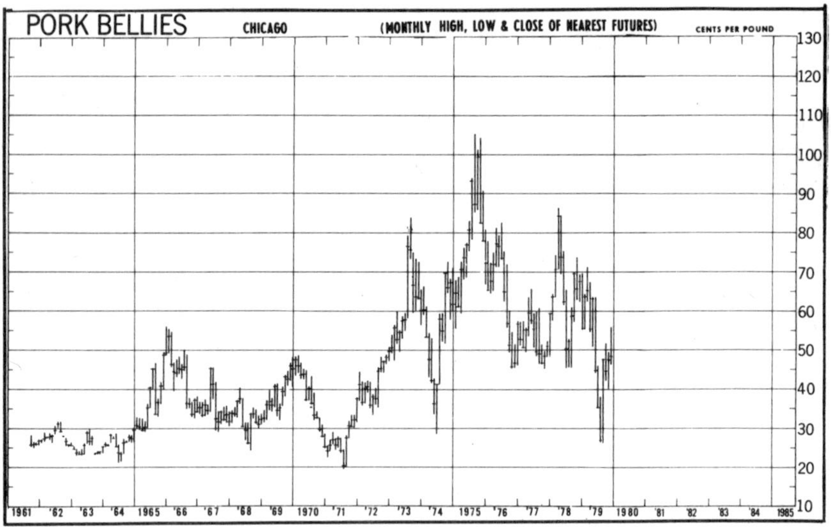

As the trader builds a file of charts over the years, many possible patterns in price movements become apparent. You have seen in the last few illustrations the phenomenon of three or four year price cycles, when prices rise successively for a number of years and then fall just as successively in reaction. This is by no means a rigid law or an always dependable pattern. It can be consulted, however, while you graph the formation of sideways channels and think about the direction of their next breakout. But don't jump ahead of the market based on an interpretation of long-range cycle patterns. As always, wait until a **real** move in prices confirms (or refutes) your analysis.

In previous examples you have seen how, sometimes, a group of related commodities can rise or fall together. When such a group move does occur, the method trader stands to make enormous profits. The same chart analysis for one commodity will work for the others, multiplying your profits without any appreciable increase in risk or effort. If each and every one of the contracts considered qualifies, through an inspection of price history and price charts, for the method of trading we have proposed, then you can go ahead and play them all. When the group price move is over, one or two of the contracts may be seen to have moved farther and faster. No one could have predicted this ahead of time. By playing them all, the trader may be reasonably assured of catching the best possible action. One golden opportunity of this kind came in the lucrative grain and soybean futures markets of 1979.

There are real world factors that tie together the prices of corn, wheat, oats, soybeans, soybean meal and soybean oil. If one commodity can be fairly easily substituted for another by users, then the prices of those commodities will be linked. The supply and demand for one will affect the supply and demand for the others. This is especially true in the so-called "feed-grain complex," for farmers will switch the grain they buy for livestock feed if the price of one alternative falls or rises sharply. (Thusa simple view, for there are differences among them, as in their protein content, but the general principle holds true.) Corn is the dominant feed grain, but if wheat is very cheap, it too becomes a feasible and attractive substitute. Soybean meal, which with soybean oil is obtained as a by-product of crushing whole soybeans, is a very high-protein component now used extensively to enrich the quality of the feed. If demand for feed is up, chances are that demand for meal will be up, and so will prices across the board in the soybean and feed grain groups. Heavy stockpiles of supply in one or more of these commodities may depress prices for all. Likewise heavy world demand for, say, wheat will put pressure on other competitive grains, and on soybeans as well.

With this sketch of interconnections in mind, take a look at the charts for the grain and soybean futures markets of 1979. Astonishing!! In contract after contract, from wheat to oats to soybean oil, an almost identical pattern (our favorite one!) shows up. What happened? A combination of forces in grain and bean supply and demand, plus a supportive set of long-term price cycles, came together momentarily to offer wide-awake traders a bonanza. Wheat had retraced its 1973 record high each year, until prices hit bottom in 1977. The big run-up had been partly fueled by massive Soviet purchases. World production and Russian crops increased thereafter, lowering prices. In 1978, the turnaround began. Harvest projections for the USSR began to hint at weaknesses, while a rising world standard of living continued to expand demand for the feedgrains. The Soviet decision to increase meat production ran headlong into an inefficient farm system plagued by bad weather. The record crops of 1977-1978 which

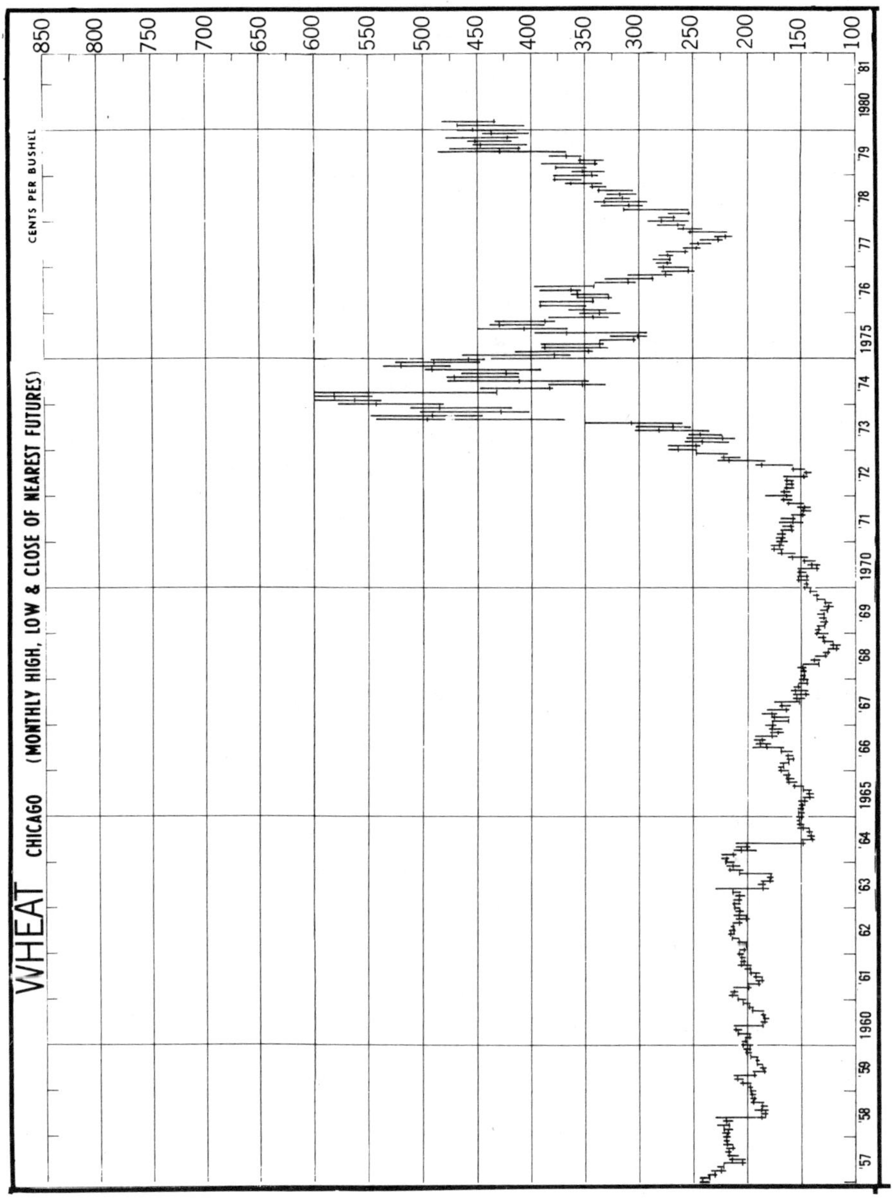
WHEAT CHICAGO (MONTHLY HIGH, LOW & CLOSE OF NEAREST FUTURES)
CENTS PER BUSHEL
850
800
750
700
650
600
550
500
450
400
350
300
250
200
150
100
'57
'58
'59
1960
'61
'62
'63
'64
1965
'66
'67
'68
'69
1970
'71
'72
'73
'74
1975
'76
'77
'78
'79
1980
'81

had pushed prices so low helped keep them relatively stable through 1978 and early into 1979.

1978-1979, however, showed a falling back from the record harvests of the season before. Rumors began to circulate about a possibly disastrous decline in the upcoming Soviet wheat crop. Thoughts went back to the spectacular bull markets of 1972-1973. On June 8, 1979, the U.S. Agriculture Department released a report officially estimating a sharp reduction in the potential 1979 Soviet grain harvest. If it held up, that estimate would mean another round of large purchases of American wheat and grains by the Soviets, and higher prices across the board for these related commodities.

The race was on. Prices on the news shot up fantastically in just a few weeks' time, shattering one long-established sideways channel after another. Farmers held crops back from the market as they hoped for even higher prices, thus turning the bull market into a self-fulfilling prophecy. Volume and open interest on the futures exchanges increased dramatically as traders flocked to join the profitable bulls, or make their fortunes as bears when the prices settled back again. But the upward move in wheat prices was dampened by another USDA report, this one showing U.S. wheat supplies in 1979 at 2.1 billion bushels, 17 percent above the 1.8 billion bushels of 1978. In the following months prices bounced up and down in a wide range as both export forecasts and crop predictions fluctuated considerably. Then came the embargo on all grain sales to the Soviet Union in early 1980, and this particular episode in the grain markets came to an end.

How could you have made a killing on these ups and downs in the grains and soybean complex? Following our method, charts for corn and wheat would have shown a narrow trading range developing around August, 1978 and continuing 1979. This would have signalled you to watch the charts for the other related commodities, checking both nearby and distant contracts in each of the commodities for the one exhibiting the most profitable price pattern. Between August of 1978 and March of 1979, easily recognizable sideways channels were formed in some contract month for corn, oats, soybeans, soybean meal and soybean oil. In the case of wheat, you could also trade contracts with narrow trading channels at the Minneapolis and Kansas City exchanges, as well as at Chicago. This would make a total of 8 different futures contract markets, all traded simultaneously through a single principle and uniform mode of analysis. Smith could simply have drawn in the narrow trading channels, set stop-orders to buy above the trading ranges, planned the stop-loss orders to trail, and then sat patiently back to wait for the move.

In corn, oats, and the soybean complex, a first move started in February. This small upward jump resulted in the formation of another general sideways trading channel. Wheat set off the second, big move in April, taking the others with it at a time lag of about a month. You were now in the game for real. Let us be conservative, and say that you traded only one contract in each commodity, and only one contract month of that commodity, for a total of 8 contracts. You would have bought corn and oil in January, wheat in April, oats in May, and soybeans and soybean meal in June. As long as the charts were accurate and the stop-orders and stop-loss orders set, you didn't have to worry about which commodity was really behind the big move, or which would go the farthest. You had them all covered. How would the results have looked?

MAXIMUM PROFITS: GRAINS AND SOYBEAN COMPLEX, 1979

Commodity	*Bought*	*Sold*	*Profit Per Contract*	*Margin*
Wheat (Chicago) Dec. '79	$3.45	$5.10	$8,250	$1,000
Wheat (K.C.) Sept. '79	$3.25	$4.75	$7,500	$1,000
Wheat (MPLS) Sept. '79	$3.25	$4.75	$7,500	$1,000
Soybeans Jan. '80	$7.30	$8.40	$5,500	$1,200
Soy. Meal Dec. '79	$200	$230	$3,000	$1,200
Soy. Oil Dec. '79	$24.4¢	29.2¢	$2,880	$1,200
Corn Dec. '79	$2.56	$3.26	$3,500	$ 600
Oats Sept. '79	$1.60	$1.84	$1,200	$ 500
		TOTALS	$39,330	$7,700

RETURN ON INVESTMENT: 510%

Even if one were to subtract a full twenty percent from this maximum profit as an allowance for commissions, poor executions, and exits from the market after the reversal was underway, total profits would still be $31,470 or 408 percent of the initial margin requirement. What other investment medium that is both rational and legal offers you a 400 percent return on your investment in less than five months time?

1980 began as the most spectacular year in commodity futures trading since the grain markets of 1972-1973 first brought international fame to the speculative trade. The history books had to be re-written once more as the prices of the "precious metals" — gold, silver, platinum, even copper

— soared to heights undreamed of even by the most ardent bull trader. Metals earned their reputation as the most dangerous game in futures trading. When it was all over and the dust had settled, even multi-billionaires found that you could be ruined by not respecting the decisions of the marketplace.

The upward climb of metals prices had been slow but generally steady since 1976, with gold outperforming slower moving markets in silver and platinum. During the 1970s, many factors drew together to attract new, high-stakes players to the futures markets in metals. Growing global economic and political crises prompted everyone from the retired pensioner to the Arab oil sheik to seek a hedge against chaos and inflation. The final separation of silver and gold as commodities from U.S. and other monetary systems created the conditions for a speculative surge. Old style fundamentals like mine output and industrial use, though still influential, were overshadowed by the new set of economic and political fundamentals: the metals markets became an international barometer of global tensions and fears. At the same time, a small group of "silver bulls" led by the super-wealthy Hunt family of Texas accelerated their program of enormous speculation in silver futures and massive hoarding of silver bullion.

In the fall of 1979, a crowd of Iranians stormed the United States embassy in Tehran and took some 50 Americans hostage. International political anxieties mounted daily as the unprecedented crisis dragged on. American "war fever," the increasing nervousness of Arab investors who feared similar events in their own countries, and a certain amount of simple market hysteria and human greed sent metals prices into the stratosphere, far beyond the range of their traditional and historic ratio to other prices in the economy. Exchange and brokerage officials scrambled to control the situation in

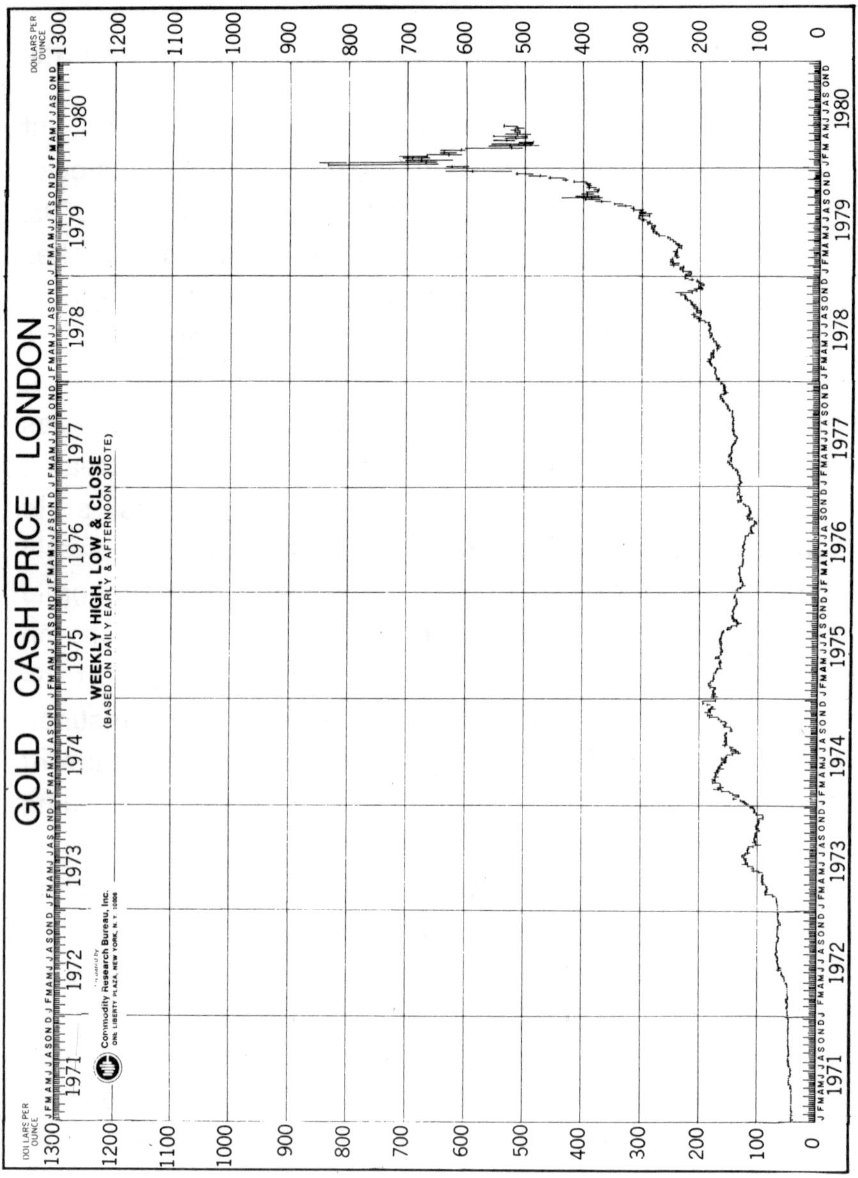
GOLD CASH PRICE LONDON
WEEKLY HIGH, LOW & CLOSE
(BASED ON DAILY EARLY & AFTERNOON QUOTE)
Commodity Research Bureau, Inc.
ONE LIBERTY PLAZA, NEW YORK, N.Y. 10006
DOLLARS PER OUNCE
1300
1200
1100
1000
900
800
700
600
500
400
300
200
100
0
1971
1972
1973
1974
1975
1976
1977
1978
1979
1980

the face of sensational publicity and government criticism. One of the rules of the game was that the rules of the game could be changed in the middle of the game, if the exchange so deemed it necessary. Many long-time traders, some of them prominent members of the exchanges, had been caught on the wrong side when prices exploded. To slow the trade and limit volatility, margin requirements were raised so high in response (reaching over $75,000 per contract in gold and silver) that all but the most wealthy were effectively shut out of the market. Limits on new positions were imposed, and these with other measures helped precipitate the wholesale collapse of the silver market and the big fall back in gold and platinum. Without sufficient new numbers of buyers, bull traders could not continue driving prices up. The foundation (if there had been any real one in the first place) for high prices disappeared, and prices went back through the floor. Some traders who had kept on buying at very high levels found themselves wiped out when the reverse came.

These were not easy markets to trade, especially after the big moves were well underway. But the calm, careful method trader could have caught the moves in gold, silver and platinum back in the middle of August, 1979 when margins were still low and markets liquid. Then it was a matter of skill, luck, and a bit of daring to hold on during the October-November fluctuations and into the dramatic peak period. Here greed would have destroyed the position, as too many new contracts bought at high prices would more than offset gains made on the first contracts. These were generally not markets for those with limited means, unless they got on board early, traded conservatively, and took profits reasonably. Still, in all, it could be done and **it was done** by many average speculators.

Gold: The October 1980 contract penetrated the $350

ceiling in August, 1979, signalling a buy at that price. Contract high came in January of 1980 at $940, a profit of $59,000 per contract. Limit moves and extreme volatility would have hampered the trader trying to exit the market, however, so a more reasonable point at which to expect liquidation would be about $750. There, profit would still have been $40,000 per contract (margin in the first half of 1979 was $1000 per contract).

Silver: The August 1980 contract broke the ceiling of $10 in both July and August of 1979. That was the time to buy. Silver topped out early in 1980 at $43, a maximum profit of $151,500 per contract. A more reasonable exit estimate might put liquidation around $37.00. Profit at that level would have been $135,000 per contract (margin in early 1979 was $2000 per contract).

Platinum: The move in April 1980 Platinum began in earnest in September of 1979. The method trader would have bought at $440, and watched prices climb to a record of $1,020. A reasonable exit would have been near $880, for a profit of $22,000 per contract (early 1979 margin was $1,500).

The economic pressures of 1980 gave the trader numerous other outstanding profit opportunities in less tumultuous markets. Record high interest rates designed to slow inflation caused a complete collapse in the market for long-term U.S. Treasury Bonds. June 1980 contracts paid a maximum of $26,000 per contract on a $3000 margin. Spurred by poor global harvest predictions, and by renewed speculative interest, sugar performed magnificently, bringing the method trader a maximum of $30,240 per contract on a $2000 margin. High oil prices began to lessen the attraction of synthetic fabrics demanding petroleum for their production, while textile manufacturing continued to expand in the underdeveloped nations. Result: profit on the May 1980 Cotton contract was $10,000 on a $1000 margin.

III

What does the future hold for commodity futures trading? The evidence of history, in case after documented case, strongly suggests that identical trading opportunities to those you have already seen will occur, year in and year out, for as long as futures markets exist. The trading principles and methods you have learned, and seen illustrated, in this book will apply throughout the coming years. With them you will be able to trade new contracts as well as old, at any exchange, as long as you proceed carefully and according to the rules.

What year is it today? 1982? 1988? 1995? 2001? No matter. The patterns you have taught yourself to recognize are there for you to profit by. Individual commodities and individual contracts may come and go, but the basic principles of successful futures speculation will never fundamentally change. Indeed, the central lesson of the method we have been examining is that the trading pattern occurs **regardless** of the type of commodity or the year it is traded. The method trader is watching for price patterns, specific kinds of price movements. If considerations of other kinds are given too much weight, the trader can be easily led astray, instead of following the actual movement of prices as the market determines them.

To prove the point to yourself, go down to your broker's office today and borrow or copy a set of price charts for the last year or so. Look through these charts keeping in mind the

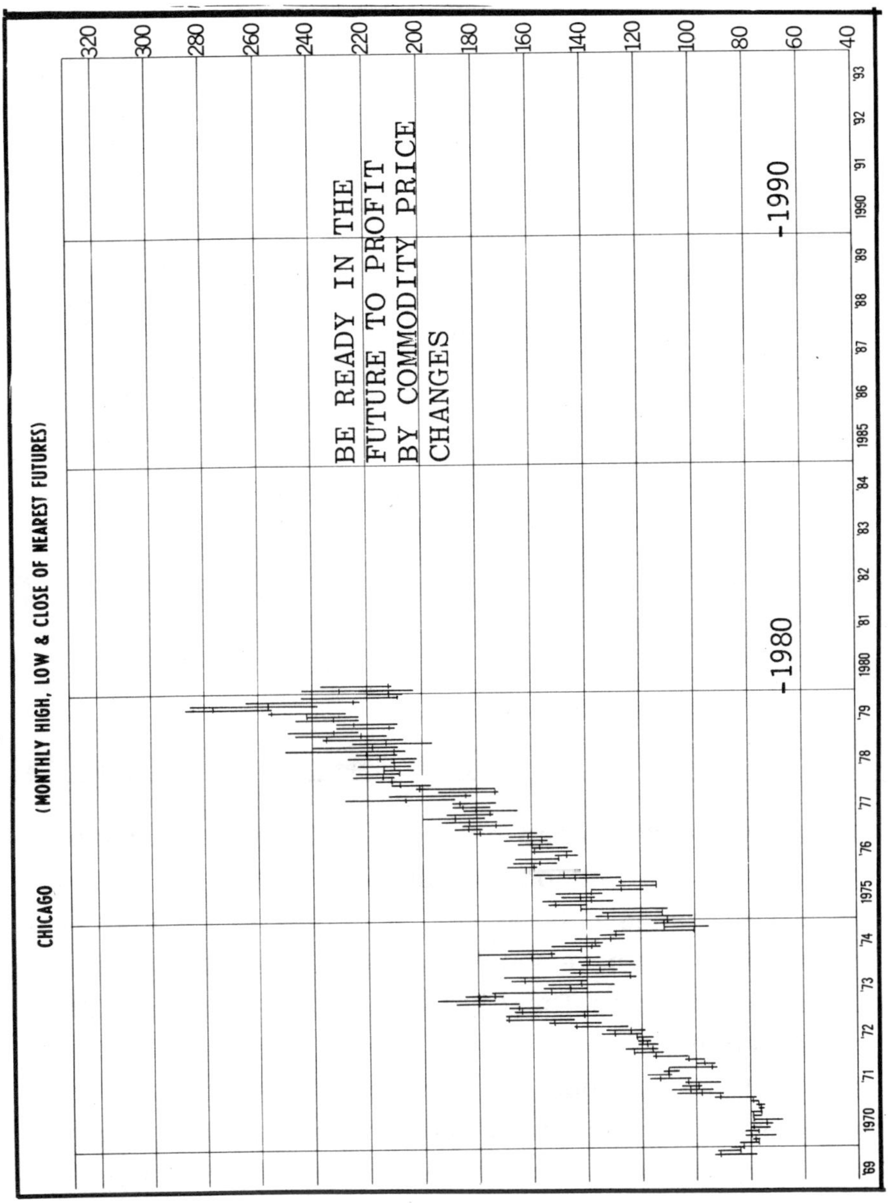
CHICAGO
(MONTHLY HIGH, LOW & CLOSE OF NEAREST FUTURES)
BE READY IN THE
FUTURE TO PROFIT
BY COMMODITY PRICE
CHANGES
-1980
-1990
320
300
280
260
240
220
200
180
160
140
120
100
80
60
40
'69
1970
'71
'72
'73
'74
1975
'76
'77
'78
'79
1980
'81
'82
'83
'84
1985
'86
'87
'88
'89
1990
'91
'92
'93

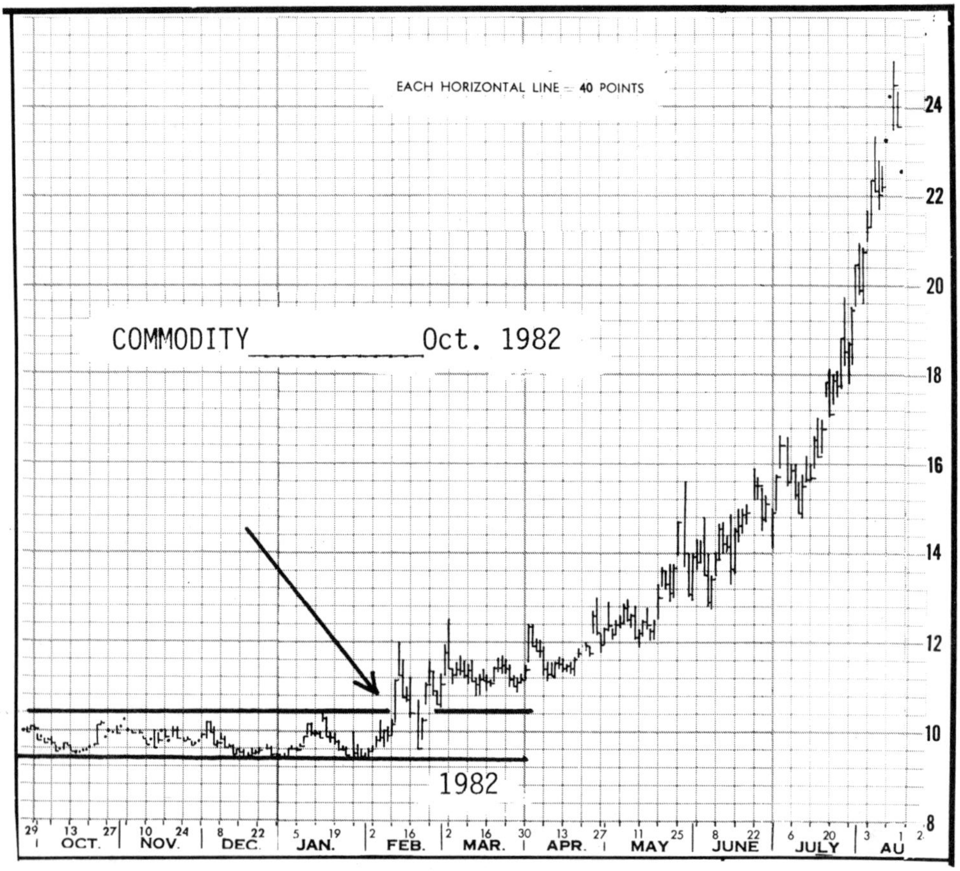

lessons you have learned in the last two chapters. Examining the charts, you will doubtlessly find the same kinds of sideways channels, breakouts, and upward or downward price moves that have shown themselves regularly since the beginning of trading. These are the constantly repeating price patterns that continually present knowledgeable traders with excellent profit opportunities, whether the contract be in soybeans or moon rocks, whether the exchange be in Chicago, London, or the Milky Way. Prices can still only go one of three ways — up, down, or sideways, and as long as that is so, the speculator will have many chances to make a fortune in commodities.

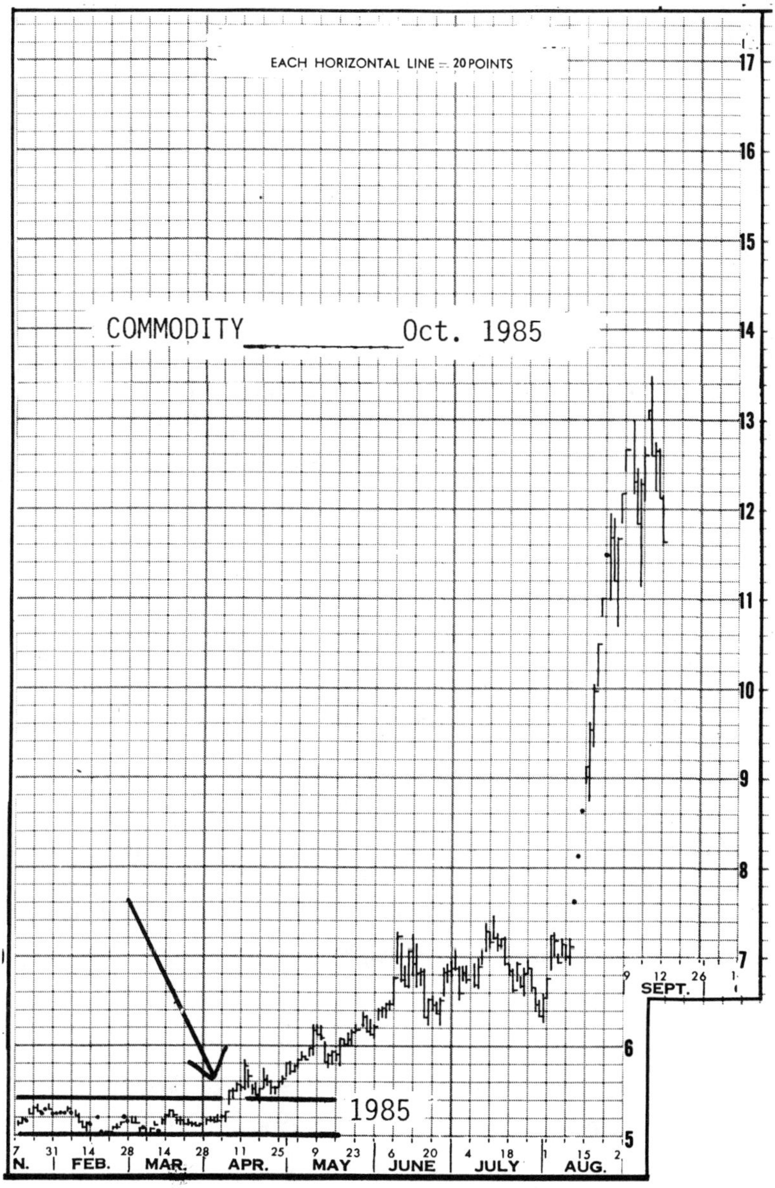

THE PATTERN YOU HAVE STUDIED WILL BE REPEATED, YEAR IN AND YEAR OUT, AS LONG AS THERE ARE FUTURES MARKETS.

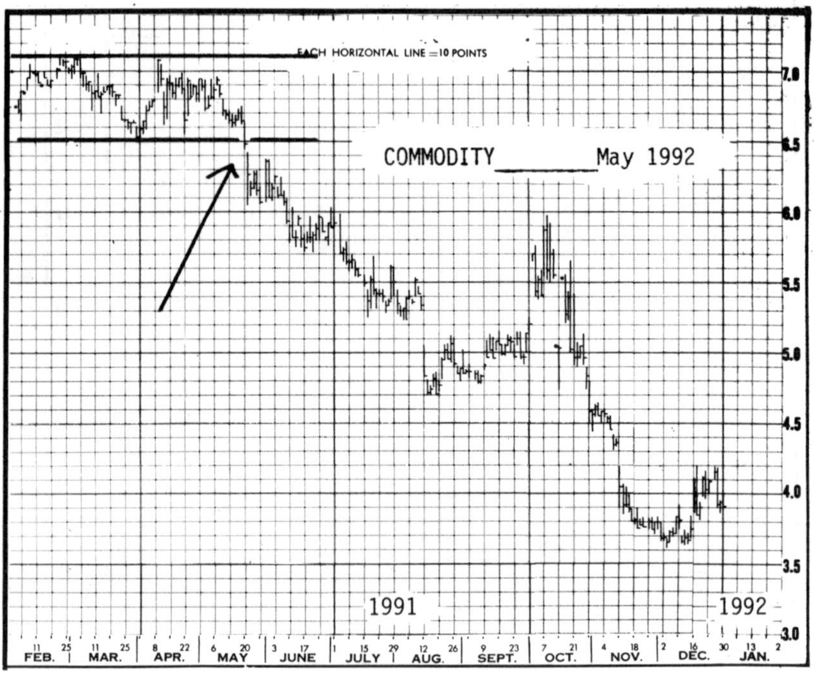

Take a look at the charts on these and the following pages. They are examples of the types of opportunities you can expect to discover in your own day, and in the future. The names of the commodities have been left blank, and the years are hypothetical, but the odds are that each and every one will soon be repeated. Comparing your own charts for recent years with these models, you'll be able to fill in the blank where the commodity's name belongs, as you spot and profit by movements just like these. You will see how many fabulous opportunities have arisen since this book was written and published, how many times you could have made 500 or 5,000 percent on your investment. Don't let the future in

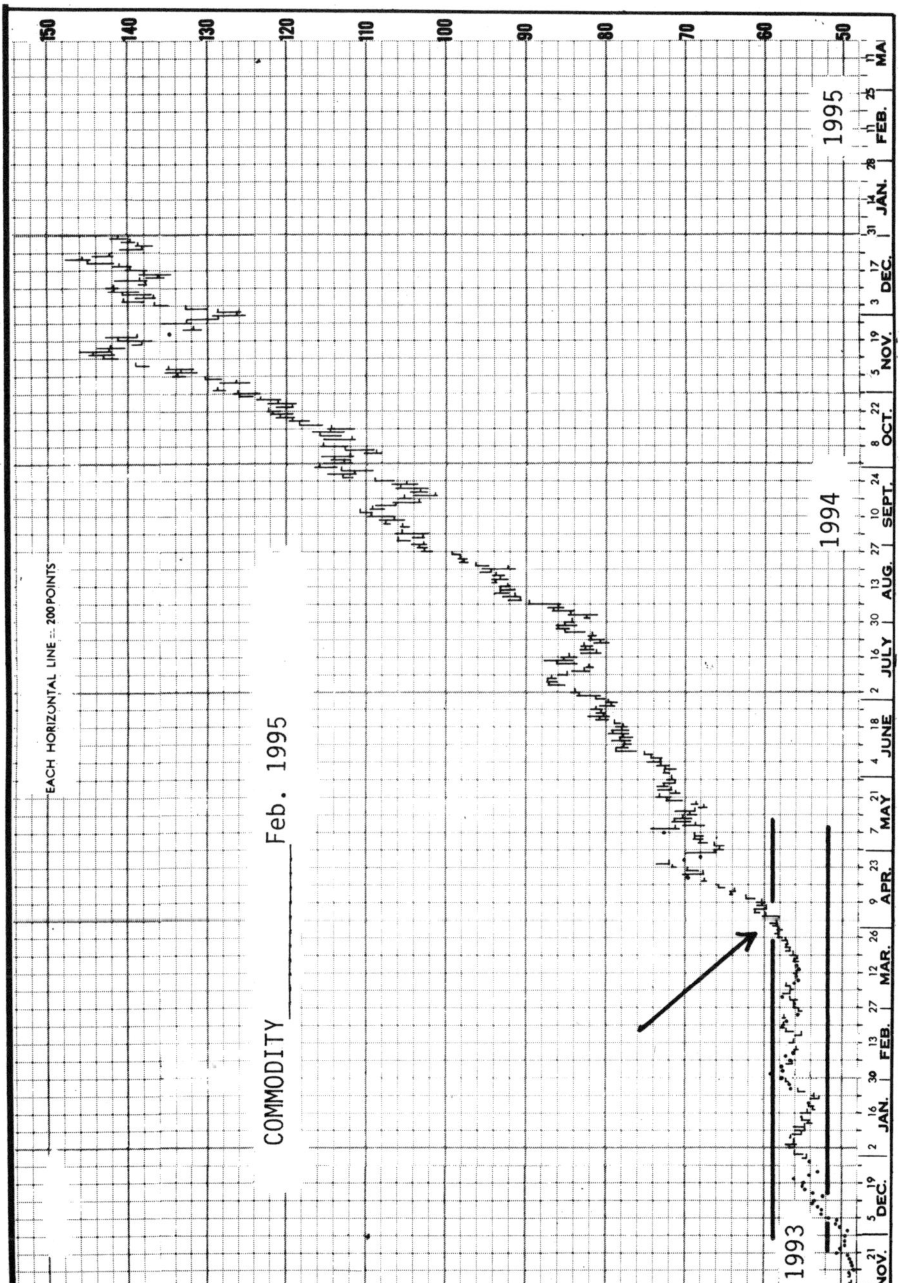
EACH HORIZONTAL LINE = 200 POINTS
COMMODITY
Feb. 1995
1993
1994
1995
150
140
130
120
110
100
90
80
70
60
50
NOV. DEC. JAN. FEB. MAR. APR. MAY JUNE JULY AUG. SEPT. OCT. NOV. DEC. JAN. FEB. MA

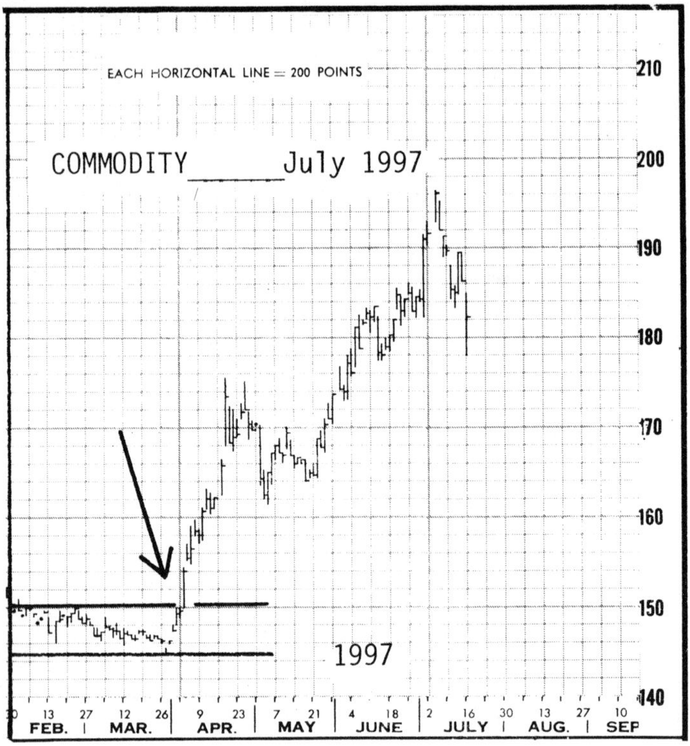

futures get away from you. The future is **now.** Somewhere, in some commodity, a price pattern is forming **now** that conforms to our model and offers you very handsome rewards.

Of course, there is far more to be said about futures trading and speculation than has thus far been covered. In your reading, in examining the charts, and in actually playing the futures markets, many more questions arise than this book could address. What does one do if the markets turn **against** a position? Exactly how **does** the successful speculator calculate the placement of stop-loss orders? How important is price forecasting, as opposed to just playing the price chart? Are there **other** recurrent chart formations that can be traded methodically and profitably? Do cash prices determine futures prices, or do futures prices determine cash

prices? What are the various kinds of orders I can use to ensure accurate execution of my trade? How quickly should the losing trader exit from a bad position? Where can the speculator find out about the supply and demand situation for a particular commodity? What are the odds that a particular commodity will rise, or fall, in prices during the summer as opposed to the spring? Is it best to trade one or two commodities? Ten? Thirty? Should a broker be allowed to trade the account at his or her own discretion? Are some commodities consistently more volatile than others? What difference does the amount of volume or open interest make to the success of a trade? How much should I be paying in commissions? How much should I have in liquid capital and net assets **before** I start trading commodity futures?

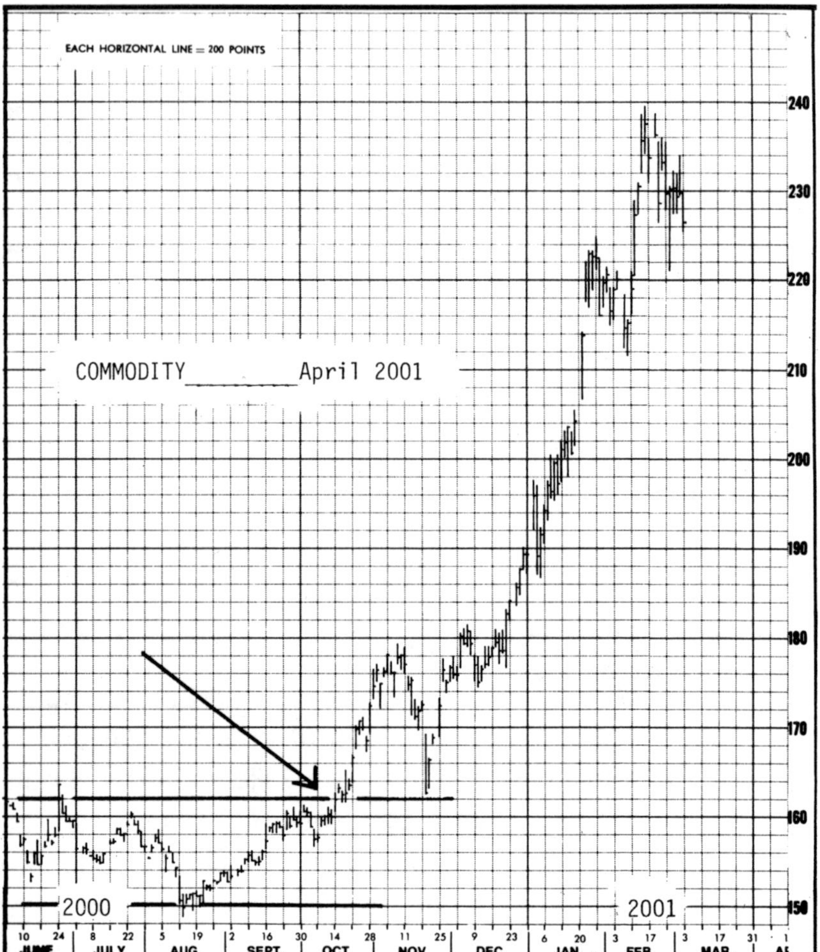

SUCCESSFUL COMMODITY FUTURES TRADING IS A SKILL THAT LASTS A LIFETIME.

These are just some of the hundreds of questions I have been asked during my years as a commodity trader and advisor. They occur to everyone entering the field of futures speculation. This book, however, was not meant to be exhaustive: it is only an introduction to futures trading and a handbook for one method to successfully make a fortune in commodities. I have written a number of other books, and thousands of pages of newsletters, in answer to questions like those above. These materials cover everything from the ancient history of futures trading up through today's most sophisticated systems for futures speculation. Those of you who want to continue your investigations of futures trading may be interested in:

***The Dow Jones-Irwin Guide To Commodities Trading.** (New, revised edition). A nationwide financial best-seller, the **Guide** is a complete, exhaustive and thorough presentation of all important aspects of the futures business. Its simple, clear explanations make it an ideal introductory text, while its philosophy of trading and system of price analysis are of great value to the most experienced of traders. It's coverage includes the basic mechanics of trading, the choice of a brokerage firm, the economics of both cash and futures pricing, the individual fundamentals for all the major commodities, the construction of a trading plan and the management of the individual commodity account.

*****The Commodity Trading Manual.** Praised by thousands as the single most valuable book in the business, the *Manual* provides detailed instructions in 7 different trading methods that are proven winners. Plain English and common sense spell out a step-by-step program for developing a rational, profitable trading plan. Learn what records to keep, how to figure the odds, how to exit and enter with the least risk, how to maximize profits and cut losses. A priceless aid for the serious commodity trader.

*****"Bruce Gould On Commodities."** Since 1976, "Bruce Gould On Commodities" has provided subscribers world-wide with informed commentary on current markets and trading strategies. This unique, bi-weekly newsletter combines a review of major markets with a continuing series of articles on the principles, systems, theories and practices of commodity futures trading. (Back issues are available.)

*****"Bruce Gould Daily."** The ultimate service for the commodity futures speculator. Each and every day after the close of the futures exchanges, **specific** position recommendations are tape-recorded and made available to subscribers through a telephone "hot-line." Recommendations include general trends, which markets to play long and which to play short, and **exact** stop-order and stop-loss points for those commodities considered the best bets.

For more information, **simply return one of the post-cards provided at the back of this book.** Or write to me personally: **Bruce Gould, P.O. Box 16, Seattle, WA 98111.**

I have dedicated my career as a commodity trading advisor to one foremost goal: to give the average person a good chance to make substantial profits in futures trading, and I believe I have succeeded. Good luck with your trading, and if I can be of any help to you personally, don't hesitate to write.

Respectfully submitted,

Dr. Bruce Grant Gould

APPENDIX I:
ESTIMATED VALUE OF COMMODITIES TRADED

ESTIMATED "VALUE" OF COMMODITIES TRADED 1960 THROUGH 1980

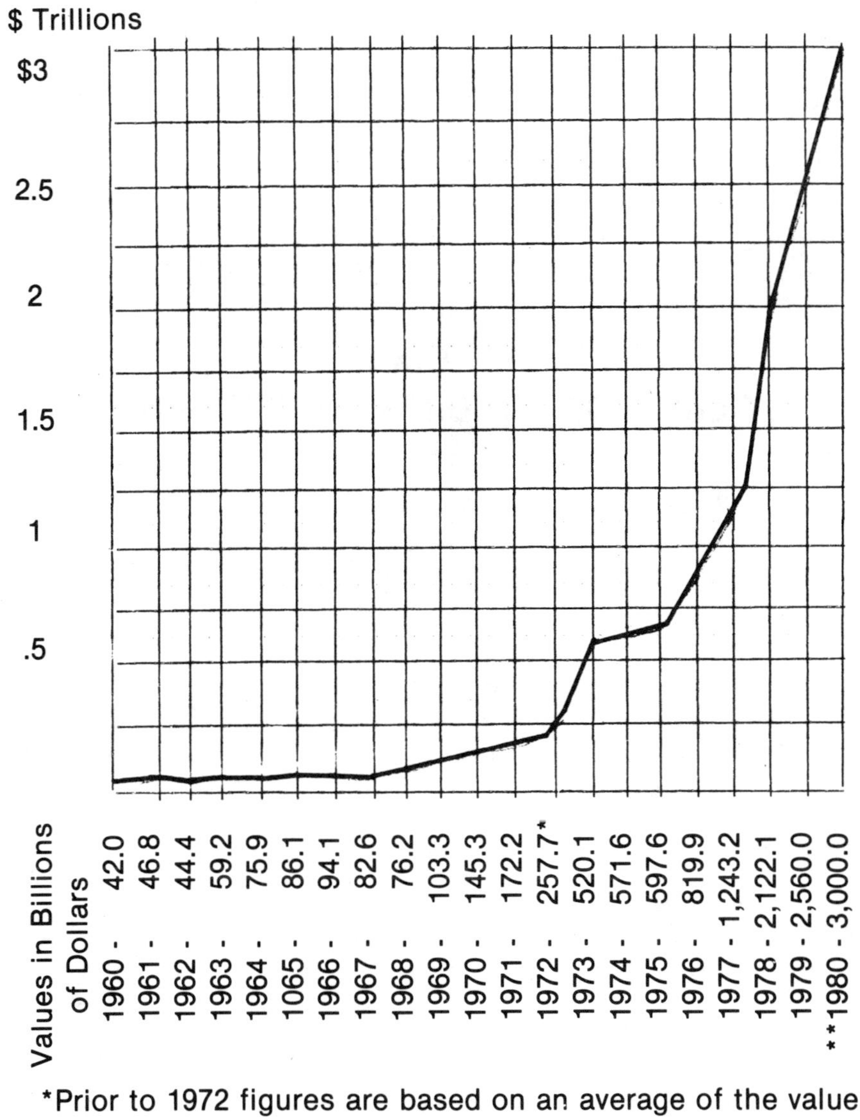

*Prior to 1972 figures are based on an average of the value of commodities traded and reported on a fiscal basis.

**Estimated

Source: Futures Industry Association

APPENDIX II: VOLUME OF TRADING IN FUTURES

VOLUME OF TRADING IN FUTURES
1957 THROUGH 1980

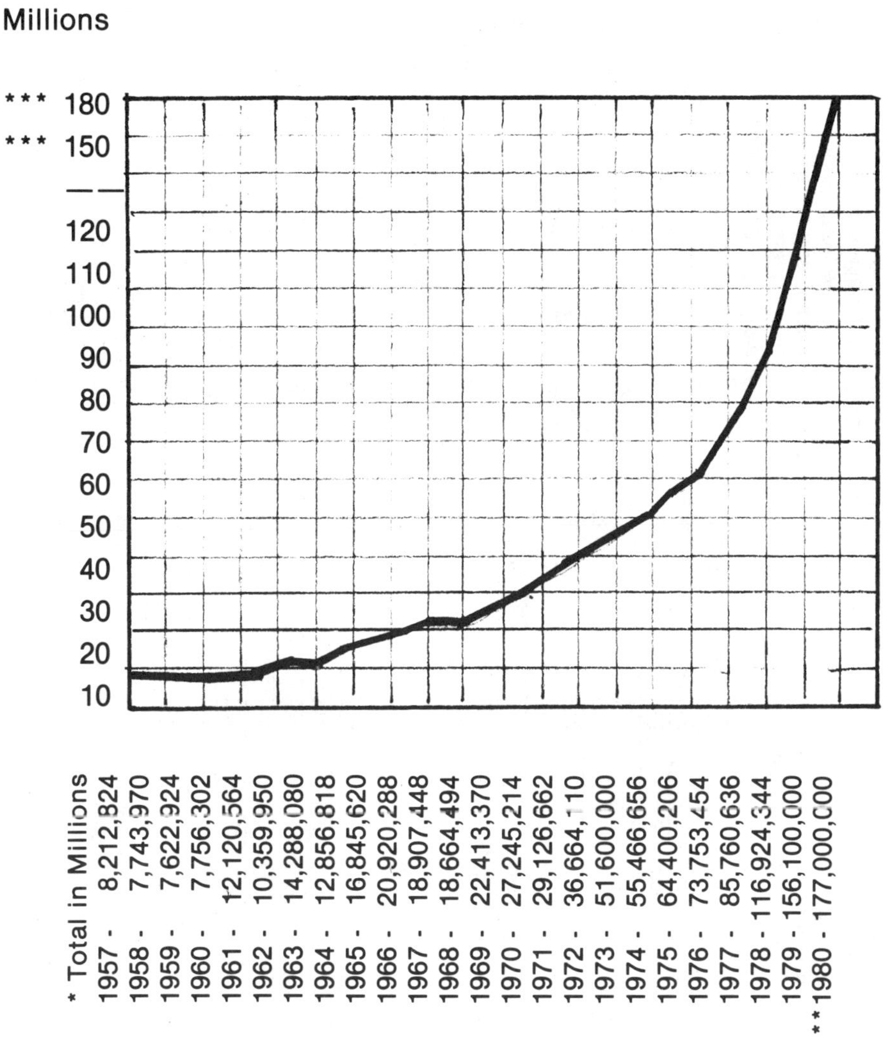

*Totals - Number of Trades (Buys plus Sells) - i.e. Number of Contracts traded times two.

**Estimated

***Note change of scale

Source: Futures Industry Association

Trading Volume The following table shows estimated volume of futures trading, all commodities and major groups, annually, 1960, 1970, 1974-78 and monthly for 1978, by number of contracts.

Year or Mo.	All Commodities	Grains & Feeds[1]	Livestock & Meat[2]	Foods[3]	Raw Materials[4]	Precious Metals[5]	Financial[6] Instruments	Currencies[7]
				Number of Contracts				
1960	3,878,151	2,411,026	8,364	1,288,878	169,429	454	0	0
1970	13,355,940	5,977,433	2,573,740	3,457,726	350,728	994,973	0	1,340
1974	27,733,328	13,419,642	4,628,990	4,153,871	1,464,781	3,826,407	0	239,637
1975	32,200,170	14,595,037	5,680,175	3,691,553	1,609,108	6,375,711	20,125	228,461
1976	36,875,727	17,260,819	5,324,961	3,868,357	2,775,963	7,209,314	238,791	197,522
1977	42,847,064	19,668,086	5,666,370	5,161,032	2,753,110	8,232,260	779,778	586,428
1978P	58,430,813	22,366,326	9,656,452	5,146,317	3,396,659	13,979,290	2,325,020	1,560,749
1978								
Jan	3,878,561	1,416,994	549,210	398,595	228,316	1,117,346	98,802	69,298
Feb	3,438,457	1,178,426	672,182	365,604	241,476	820,280	82,487	78,002
Mar	5,704,265	2,468,187	915,919	522,665	284,730	1,295,144	105,845	111,775
Apr	4,815,394	2,174,541	814,423	458,259	258,307	876,025	119,153	114,686
May	4,756,790	2,038,173	1,002,194	398,206	279,865	787,691	125,606	125,055
Jun	4,885,643	2,081,075	958,110	463,567	309,342	789,335	157,637	126,577
Jul	4,182,934	1,674,831	771,437	365,782	221,272	851,969	152,163	145,480
Aug	5,266,122	1,859,458	781,164	458,941	324,096	1,393,442	247,354	201,667
Sept	4,435,780	1,495,230	777,093	419,274	256,247	1,094,203	249,856	143,877
Oct	6,230,774	2,275,745	931,554	500,213	360,453	1,634,810	309,329	218,670
Nov	5,863,708	2,105,192	751,093	429,567	369,616	1,728,313	351,822	128,105
Dec	4,972,385	1,598,474	732,073	365,644	262,939	1,590,732	324,966	97,557

P Preliminary Source: Futures Industry Association

[1]Wheat, corn, oats, rye, soybeans, soybean meal, grain sorghums. [2]Cattle, feeder cattle, hogs, pork bellies, frozen boneless beef, broilers, turkeys. [3]Eggs, potatoes, coffee, cocoa, sugar, butter orange juice, pepper, apples, edible oils (soybean, cottonseed, coconut, palm). [4] Lumber, stud lumber, plywood, cotton, wool, oil and petroleum products, copper, lead, mercury, zinc, nickel, rubber, tin. [5]Gold, silver, silver coins, platinum, palladium. [6]GNMA, treasury bills and bonds, commercial paper. [7]Italian Lira, Mexican Pesos, Canadian Dollars, French Francs, Deutschemarks, Dutch Guilders, British Pounds, Japanese Yen, Swiss Francs, Belgian Francs.

APPENDIX III: CONTRACT MARKET DESIGNATIONS

CONTRACT MARKET DESIGNATIONS

Commodity	Exchange[1]	Effective date[2] of designation	Trading[3] begun
Previously Regulated Agricultural Commodities			
Wheat	MACE	Oct. 24, 1922	Prior to 1880
	MGE	May 2, 1923	Jan. 2, 1885
	CBOT	May 3, 1923	1877
	KCBT	May 5, 1923	Jan. 2, 1877
Durum	MGE	May 2, 1923	Oct. 31, 1973
Corn	MACE	Oct. 24, 1922	Prio to 1880
	MGE	May 2, 1923	Jan. 30, 1922
	CBOT	May 3, 1923	1877
	KCBT	May 5, 1923	Jan. 2, 1877
Oats	MACE	Oct. 24, 1922	Prior to 1880
	MGE	May 2, 1923	Jan. 2, 1918
	CBOT	May 3, 1923	1877
Rye	MGE	May 2, 1923	Jan. 3, 1918
Barley	MGE	May 2, 1923	Oct. 9, 1918
Grain Sorghums	KCBT	May 5, 1923	Jan. 29, 1916
	CME	Jan. 27, 1971	Mar. 2, 1971
Soybeans	CBOT	Dec. 8, 1940	Oct. 5, 1936
	MACE	Dec. 8, 1940	Oct. 5, 1936
	MGE	Sept. 11, 1950	Sept. 20, 1950
	KCBT	Sept. 10, 1956	Sept. 18, 1956
Soybean Meal	CBOT	Aug. 22, 1951	Aug. 19, 1951
Soybean Oil	CBOT	June 30, 1950	July 17, 1950
Flaxseed	MGE	May 2, 1923	July 2, 1920
Cotton	Cotton	Sept. 13, 1936	Sept. 10, 1870
Eggs	CME	Sept. 13, 1936	Dec. 1, 1919
Butter	CME	Sept. 13, 1936	Dec. 1, 1919
Potatoes	CME	Sept. 13, 1936	Jan. 12, 1931
	NYME	Dec. 1, 1941	Dec. 1, 1941
Frozen concentrated orange juice	Citrus	July 24, 1968	Oct. 26, 1966
Cattle			
Live beef	CME	June 18, 1968	Nov. 30, 1964
Live beef	MACE	Sept. 11, 1978	Sept. 28, 1978
Live feeder	CME	June 18, 1968	Nov. 30, 1971
Frozen boneless beef	CME	Mar. 13, 1970	April, 1970
Imported lean beef	NYME	Aug. 11, 1971	Sept. 15, 1971
Live Hogs	CME	June 18, 1968	Feb. 28, 1966
	MACE	Sept. 14, 1973	June 3, 1974
Frozen pork bellies	CME	June 18, 1968	Sept. 18, 1961
	MGE	Mar. 19, 1971	April 5, 1971
Frozen skinned hams	CME	July 19, 1968	Feb. 3, 1964
Newly Regulated Agricultural and Forest Produce Commodities			
Turkeys	CME	July 18, 1975	Oct. 1, 1945
Iced Broilers	CBOT	July 18, 1975	Aug. 1, 1968
Plywood	CBOT	July 18, 1975	Dec. 1, 1969
Stud Lumber	CBOT	July 18, 1975	Dec. 1, 1972
	CME	Oct. 4, 1977	Dec. 1, 1977
Lumber	CME	July 18, 1975	Oct. 1, 1969

Commodity	Exchange[1]	Effective date[2] of designation	Trading[3] begun
International Commodities			
Cocoa	Cocoa	July 18, 1975	Oct. 1, 1925
Rubber	Cocoa	July 18, 1975	Jan. 22, 1975
Coffee	NYC&S	July 18, 1975	March 7, 1882
Sugar	NYC&S	July 18, 1975	Dec. 16, 1914
Metals			
Silver	CBOT	July 18, 1975	Nov. 3, 1969
	Comex	July 18, 1975	July 5, 1933
	MACE	July 18, 1975	Oct. 1968
U.S. Silver Coins	CME	July 18, 1975	Oct. 1, 1973
	MACE	July 18, 1975	Mar. 27, 1972
	NYME	July 18, 1975	April 1, 1971
Copper	Comex	July 18, 1975	July 5, 1933
	CME	July 18, 1975	July 1, 1974
Gold	CBOT	July 18, 1975	Dec. 31, 1974
	Comex	July 18, 1975	Dec. 31, 1974
	CME	July 18, 1975	Dec. 31, 1974
	MACE	July 18, 1975	Dec. 31, 1974
	NYME(kilo)	July 18, 1975	Dec. 31, 1974
	(400 oz.)	Oct. 18, 1977	Nov. 14, 1977
Palladium	NYME	July 18, 1975	Jan. 22, 1968
Platinum	CME	July 19, 1977	Aug. 1977
	NYME	July 18, 1975	Dec. 3, 1956
Zinc	Comex	Oct. 4, 1977	Feb. 8, 1978
Currencies			
Canadian Dollars	CME	July 18, 1975	May 16, 1972
	NYME	July 18, 1975	Sept. 12, 1974
Deutsche Mark	CME	July 18, 1975	May 16, 1972
	NYME	July 18, 1975	Sept. 12, 1974
Dutch Guilders	CME	July 18, 1975	May 16, 1972
	NYME	July 18, 1975	Sept. 12, 1974
French Francs	CME	July 18, 1975	Sept. 23, 1974
Japanese Yen	CME	July 18, 1975	May 16, 1972
	NYME	July 18, 1975	Sept. 12, 1974
Mexican Peso	CME	July 18, 1975	May 16, 1972
	NYME	July 18, 1975	Sept. 12, 1974
British Pound Sterling	CME	July 18, 1975	May 16, 1972
Swiss Francs	CME	July 18, 1975	May 16, 1972
	NYME	July 18, 1975	Sept. 12, 1974
Belgian Franc	NYME	July 18, 1975	Sept. 12, 1974
British Pound	NYME	July 18, 1975	Sept. 12, 1974
Italian Lira	NYME	July 18, 1975	Sept. 12, 1974
Financial Instruments			
Commercial Paper Loans (90 day)	CBOT	July 12, 1977	Sept. 26, 1977
GNMA Mortgages	CBOT	Sept. 1,1 1975	Oct. 20, 1975
GNMA Mortgages (Cer. Del.)	CBOT		Sept. 12, 1978
GNMA Mortgages (Cer. Del.)	ACE	Aug. 22, 1978	Sept. 12, 1978

Commodity	Exchange[1]	Effective date[2] of designation	Trading[3] begun
Financial Instruments (Continued)			
Long Term U.S. Treasury Bonds (15 years)	CBOT	Aug. 2, 1977	Aug. 22, 1977
U.S. Treasury Bills (90 days)	CME	Nov. 26, 1975	Jan. 6, 1976
U.S. Treasury Bills (1 year)	CME	Aug. 25, 1978	Sept. 11, 1978
Petroleum Products			
Heating Oil (Rotterdam)	NYME	July 18, 1975	Oct. 23, 1974
Industrial Fuel Oil (Rotterdam)	NYME	July 18, 1975	Oct. 23, 1974
Liquid Propane	Petroleum	July 18, 1975	Feb. 1, 1971
Crude Oil	Petroleum	July 18, 1975	Sept. 10, 1974

[1] The term "exchange" includes only those 11 exchanges which are designated as contract markets and presently have trading activity. The following abbreviations are used for convenience to indicate the respective exchange:

Amex Commodities Exchange, Inc.	ACE	New York Mercantile Exchange	NYME
Chicago Board of Trade	CBOT	New York Coffee & Sugar Exch.	NYC&S
Chicago Mercantile Exchange	CME	New York Cotton Exchange	Cotton
MidAmerica Commodity Exch.	MACE	Wool Associates of Cotton	Wool
Kansas City Board of Trade	KCBT	Citrus Associates of Cotton	Citrus
Minneapolis Grain Exchange	MGE	Petroleum Assoc. of Cotton	Petroleum
New York Cocoa Exchange	Cocoa	Commodity Exchange, Inc.	Comex

CME includes commodities traded on the International Monetary Market. That exchange merged with the CME on March 18, 1976.

[2] The term "effective date of designation" is the date upon which the exchange was authorized to begin trading in the contract, not the date of the issuance of the designation order.

If an exchange was previously designated by the Secretary of Agriculture as a contract market in a commodity and that designation was in effect on July 18, 1975, the Commission had not specifically designated them as such on July 18, 1975. Those designations continued in full force and effect by virtue of Section 411 of the Commodity Futures Trading Act of 1974. Prior to July 18, 1975, the commodities for which designation was granted by the Secretary of Agriculture were among the lsit of commodities explicitly set forth in section 2(a)(1) of the Commodity Exchange Act, as amended, ("Act"). (This listing was limited to the agricultural and animal or animal product commodities.)

On July 18, 1975, the Commission gave contract market designations to many of the exchanges which traded in previously unregulated commodities. *See* 41 FR 33854 (August 12, 1975). Prior to that date, the Commission had given provisional contract market designations to these exchanges on April 18, 1975 which designations were extended on May 5, 1975 to July 18, 1975. *See* 41 FR 17406 (April 18, 1975), 41 FR 19035 (May 1, 1975) and 41 FR 21769 (May 19, 1975).

The effect of the July 18, 1975 designations was to bring under Federal regulation all commodities for which a futures market was actively traded. Those previously unregulated commodities for which no contract market designation was granted on July 18, 1975, such as Comex's mercury and rubber contracts, were not permitted to continue futures trading after that date.

[3] The "trading begun" column indicates, according to data supplied by the exchanges, when trading began in a commodity.

In the case of copper, silver and zinc traded on Comex, trading was suspended for periods of time and then later resumed.

Comex silver trading was first suspended on August 9, 1934. Trading resumed on June 12, 1963. A second suspension took place on August 15, 1971. Trading resumed on August 19, 1971. In the case of Comex copper, trading was first suspended on May 5, 1941 and later resumed on July 15, 1947. A second suspension took place January 29, 1951. Trading resumed February 19, 1951. A third suspension followed on July 27, 1951. Trading resumed June 1, 1953. A fourth suspension occurred on August 15, 1971. Trading resumed on August 19, 1971. In the case of Comex zinc, trading was first suspended March 3, 1941. Trading resumed July 22, 1947. A second suspension occurred January 29, 1951. Trading resumed February 19, 1951. A third suspension followed on July 27, 1951, with a resumption of trading June 23, 1952. A fourth suspension occurred October 15, 1970, followed by a resumption of trading February 8, 1978.

[4] MACE was previously named the Chicago Open Board of Trade until its name change, which was effective November 22, 1972. On January 8, 1973, the Commodity Exchange Authority amended its previous designation orders to show the name MACE instead of Chicago Open Board of Trade. The effective date of the amended order was November 22, 1972.

[5] KCBT operated as an unincorporated association until it incorporated in 1973. The CEA designated KCBT a contract market in those commodities for which the association was previously designated, the effective date of the designation being July 1, 1973.

APPENDIX IV: FUTURES FACTS

ALL COMMODITIES BY MAJOR GROUPS

Average Open Interest (in contracts)

Average Monthend	Total	Grain and Grain Products	Livestock, Livestock Products and Poultry	Foods	Industrial Raw Materials	Precious Metals	Financial Instruments	Foreign Currencies
For Fiscal Year								
1960	149,356	81,687	-	50,592	17,077	N.A.	-	-
1970	348,630	159,554	47,457	59,784	17,557	64,278	-	-
1974	586,732	217,678	49,958	58,713	40,600	208,343	-	14,440
1975	602,799	226,168	53,710	58,937	39,729	203,137	-	21,118
1976	857,699	291,677	66,664	69,700	73,923	338,955	2,940	13,840
T.Q.	877,790	352,123	52,329	73,873	85,391	302,313	5,483	6,278
1977	1,111,439	362,073	76,027	88,662	84,569	471,995	17,909	10,204
1978	1,372,022	402,677	120,711	77,125	92,968	600,356	55,607	22,578
Monthend Data - FY 73								
October	1,243,884	404,149	77,718	88,144	76,673	542,744	34,112	20,344
November	1,348,703	429,151	86,346	89,842	79,891	605,551	37,538	20,384
December	1,463,817	429,039	95,082	94,430	90,543	691,714	41,555	21,454
January	1,293,928	372,976	105,868	90,124	88,489	580,775	36,786	18,910
February	1,329,869	377,260	126,085	73,666	89,017	601,261	38,423	24,157
March	1,364,729	410,100	137,702	71,901	93,518	586,181	42,655	22,672
April	1,323,343	385,848	139,803	63,288	91,914	569,710	51,037	21,743
May	1,435,908	445,273	155,199	70,644	108,271	575,122	58,240	23,159
June	1,318,521	378,773	123,091	68,750	96,610	560,709	66,671	23,917
July	1,373,374	373,896	126,486	71,285	93,787	603,217	78,016	26,687
August	1,424,307	392,917	132,665	72,652	100,259	611,751	91,369	22,694
September	1,543,865	432,756	142,476	70,763	106,647	675,539	90,885	24,799

Wheat, corn, soybeans and oats are computed as 5,000-bushes contracts.

ALL COMMODITIES BY MAJOR GROUPS

Number of Contracts Settled by Delivery

Fiscal Year	Total	Grain and Grain Products	Livestock, Livestock Products and Poultry	Foods	Industrial Raw Materials	Precious Metals	Financial Instruments	Foreign Currencies
1960	48,495	35,705	-	8,595	4,195	N.A.	-	-
1970	76,908	30,722	7,516	9,404	2,858	26,408	-	-
1974	139,602	58,579	7,448	8,570	12,090	52,072	-	843
1975	171,125	76,006	5,149	8,150	26,696	53,827	-	1,297
1976	209,302	78,823	6,103	8,354	25,083	88,221	536	2,182
T.Q.	98,565	54,106	1,561	3,725	14,930	23,149	372	722
1977	314,963	155,132	6,028	21,424	46,444	79,608	2,267	4,060
1978	313,533	108,411	5,931	15,966	37,446	131,634	5,315	8,830
Monthly Data - FY 78								
October	16,682	6,400	313	3,476	898	5,595	-	-
November	18,143	5,443	86	1,054	3,587	7,973	-	-
December	53,838	22,402	413	542	4,629	23,336	963	1,553
January	27,330	14,410	203	3,430	2,746	6,541	-	-
February	13,613	-	356	-	317	12,940	-	-
March	50,981	23,338	323	2,856	8,606	13,226	724	1,858
April	10,985	-	498	98	234	10,155	-	-
May	29,848	8,668	467	1,500	7,484	11,729	-	-
June	21,575	-	819	15	338	15,914	1,760	2,729
July	25,605	14,102	696	1,560	3,782	5,465	-	-
August	13,305	2,462	1,354	-	92	9,397	-	-
September	31,628	11,136	403	1,435	4,733	9,363	1,868	2,690

Wheat, corn, soybeans and oats are computed as 5000-bushel contracts.

GRAIN GROUP

Average Open Interest (in contracts)

Average Monthend	Total - All Grains & Grain Products	Wheat	Corn	Oats	Soybeans	Soybean Meal	Soybean Oil	Other
for Fiscal Year								
1960	81,687	18,836	13,074	5,560	26,919	5,779	7,129	4,390
1970	159,554	26,612	40,364	5,119	38,331	21,555	26,923	650
1974	217,678	41,045	68,343	3,935	51,733	22,181	30,309	132
1975	226,168	46,464	77,995	3,287	49,772	21,332	27,218	100
1976	291,677	65,655	87,886	3,158	75,338	26,018	33,608	14
T.Q.	352,123	76,988	100,395	4,320	97,178	29,010	43,937	295
1977	362,073	68,599	98,507	3,113	98,360	41,791	51,644	59
1978	402,677	67,500	132,870	4,825	103,517	44,636	49,329	-0-
Monthly Data - FY 78								
October	404,149	75,404	136,315	3,152	96,389	43,902	48,987	-0-
November	429,151	73,011	142,592	3,266	117,423	42,256	50,603	-0-
December	429,039	75,182	134,163	2,584	128,347	38,393	50,370	-0-
January	372,976	72,465	132,103	2,701	95,490	30,042	40,175	-0-
February	377,260	64,076	141,705	3,360	88,983	34,991	44,145	-0-
March	410,100	61,150	151,614	3,252	101,765	42,325	49,994	-0-
April	385,848	57,299	135,206	4,636	98,146	40,969	49,592	-0-
May	445,273	64,326	157,980	4,791	112,251	50,633	55,292	-0-
June	378,773	56,938	114,453	4,543	99,529	50,628	52,682	-0-
July	373,896	60,689	111,179	7,074	91,829	52,895	50,230	-0-
August	392,917	70,560	109,726	8,592	98,198	56,288	49,553	-0-
September	432,756	78,904	127,405	9,954	113,856	52,315	50,322	-0-

"Other" Category varies by year but may include grain sorghum, rye and flaxseed.
Contracts of wheat, corn, soybeans and oats are converted to 5,000 bushel units.

GRAIN GROUP
Number of Contracts Traded

Fiscal Year	Total - All Grains & Grain Products	Wheat	Corn	Oats	Soybeans	Soybean Meal	Soybean Oil	Other
1960	2,552,195	515,418	336,111	115,469	1,122,503	174,990	135,397	152,307
1970	5,838,881	742,756	1,300,081	107,229	1,287,067	717,604	1,672,031	12,113
1974	11,891,186	2,643,371	4,245,900	245,127	2,506,392	705,315	1,542,941	2,140
1975	13,297,832	2,863,506	4,857,477	180,166	3,135,005	824,179	1,436,263	1,236
1976	16,095,901	3,959,852	4,841,685	133,718	4,601,373	1,071,450	1,487,547	276
T.Q.	5,041,672	1,163,171	1,299,495	47,288	1,531,884	487,943	509,921	1,970
1977	20,127,703	2,685,625	4,723,709	108,567	8,042,746	2,193,064	2,373,177	815
1978	23,102,300	3,425,797	6,264,936	172,342	8,108,606	2,354,960	2,775,659	-0-
Monthly Data - FY 78								
October	1,578,623	223,915	461,139	7,072	560,965	165,410	160,122	-0-
November	2,278,364	291,969	682,590	13,294	800,483	249,135	240,893	-0-
December	1,575,092	212,580	388,182	6,803	577,925	178,797	210,805	-0-
January	1,553,006	201,132	353,404	6,325	609,494	173,142	209,509	-0-
February	1,303,241	218,926	321,148	7,557	448,612	123,614	183,384	-0-
March	2,647,171	324,047	685,929	11,994	1,036,941	275,525	312,735	-0-
April	2,333,200	338,244	655,478	16,106	842,991	213,593	266,788	-0-
May	2,184,721	302,490	638,455	13,791	781,395	190,469	258,121	-0-
June	2,250,021	326,872	635,468	19,742	765,870	224,531	277,538	-0-
July	1,800,228	322,051	503,548	21,086	547,121	191,250	215,172	-0-
August	1,987,133	371,416	537,846	24,447	609,794	207,309	236,321	-0-
September	1,611,500	292,155	401,749	24,125	527,015	162,185	204,271	-0-

"Other" Category varies by year but may include grain sorghum, rye and flaxseed.
Contracts of wheat, corn, soybeans and oats are converted to 5,000 bushel units.

GRAIN GROUP

Number of Contracts Settled by Delivery

Fiscal Year	Total - All Grains & Grain Products	Wheat	Corn	Oats	Soybeans	Soybean Meal	Soybean Oil	Other
1960	35,705	11,576	5,502	1,887	9,642	1,254	3,337	2,507
1970	30,722	5,178	5,878	4,114	9,855	3,273	1,646	778
1974	58,579	8,012	21,987	6,577	13,955	3,564	4,129	355
1975	76,006	24,550	14,824	1,114	25,864	3,331	6,088	235
1976	78,823	26,185	14,417	1,069	23,414	4,225	9,471	42
T.Q.	54,106	15,168	5,142	1,007	10,294	10,290	12,205	-0-
1977	155,132	38,322	24,160	2,231	20,827	25,407	44,159	26
1978	108,411	25,860	25,352	5,178	27,337	16,318	8,366	-0-
Monthly Data - FY 78								
October	6,400	-	-	-	-	4,143	2,257	-0-
November	5,443	-	-	-	5,443	-	-	-0-
December	22,402	10,655	5,289	842	-	4,420	1,196	-0-
January	14,410	-	-	-	10,132	1,507	2,771	-0-
February	-	-	-	-	-	-	-	-0-
March	23,388	6,508	4,569	1,032	7,239	2,302	1,738	-0-
April	-	-	-	-	-	-	-	-0-
May	8,668	2,440	1,945	1,087	1,635	1,346	215	-0-
June	-	-	-	-	-	-	-	-0-
July	14,102	3,917	7,311	901	1,626	271	76	-0-
August	2,462	-	-	-	684	1,719	59	-0-
September	11,136	2,340	6,238	1,316	578	610	54	-0-

"Other" Category varies by year but may include grain sorghum, rye and flaxseed.
Contracts of wheat, corn, soybeans and oats are converted to 5,000 bushel units.

APPENDIX V: GOVERNMENT REPORTS

GOVERNMENT REPORTS

Crop Reporting Board, U.S. Department of Agriculture

Room 0005, Washington, DC 20250

Agricultural Price Reports

Agricultural Prices (Monthly)
  Annual (June)
Crop Values (Jan.)

Field Crops and Stocks Reports

Acreage (June)
Crop Production (Monthly)
  Annual Summary (Jan.)
Field Crops—Production, Disposition and Value (Apr.)
Grain Stocks (Quarterly)
Potato Stocks (Jan., Feb., Mar., Apr., Dec.)
Potatoes and Sweetpotatoes (Aug.)
Prospective Plantings (Jan., Apr.)
Soybean Stocks (Sept.)

Livestock and Products Reports

Cattle (Jan., July)
Cattle on Feed (Monthly)
Hogs and Pigs (Quarterly)
Lamb Crop and Wool (July)
Livestock Slaughter (Monthly)
  Annual Summary (March)
Meat Animals—Production, Disposition, and Income (Apr.)
Sheep and Goats (Jan.)
Sheep and Lambs on Feed (Jan., Mar., and Nov.)
Wool and Mohair (Mar.)

Poultry and Egg Reports

Broiler Hatchery (Weekly)
Egg Products (Monthly)
Eggs, Chickens and Turkeys (Monthly)
Hatchery Production—Annual (Mar.)
Layers and Egg Production—Annual (Jan.)
Poultry—Production, Disposition and Income (Apr.)
Poultry Slaughter (Monthly)
Turkey Hatchery (Weekly)
Turkeys (Jan.)

Seed Crop Reports

Alfalfa (Oct.)
Field Seed Stocks (Aug.)
Red Clover (Oct.)
Seed Crops (Jan.)
  Annual Summary (May)
Tall Fescue—Oregon (Aug.)
Tall Fescue—Southern States (Jul.)
Timothy (Aug.)

Other Reports

Agricultural Situation (11 x yr.)
Agricultural Statistics (Annual)
Cold Storage (Monthly)
  Regional Cold Storage Holdings (Mar.)
Farm Labor (Quarterly)
Farm Numbers (Dec.)
Farm Production Expenditures (June)
Naval Stores (Monthly)
Weekly Weather & Crop Bulletins (Weekly)

U.S. Department of Agriculture, ESCS Information Staff

Publications Unit, Room 0054-South, Washington, DC 20250

Situation Reports and Supply Demand Estimates Reports

Agricultural Finance Outlook—Annual (Dec.)
Agricultural Outlook (Monthly)
Agricultural Supply and Demand (9 x yr.)
Dairy Situation (Mar., May, Aug., Oct., Dec.)
Fats & Oils Situation (Jan., Mar., Apr., June, Sept.)
Feed Situation (Feb., May, Aug., Sept., Oct., Nov.)
Livestock & Meat Situation (Monthly)
Outlook for U.S. Exports (Quarterly)
Poultry & Egg Situation (8 x yr.)
Vegetable Situation (8 x yr.)
World Agricultural Situation (July, Oct., Dec.)

Other Reports

Agricultural Economics Research (Quarterly)
Agricultural Finance Review (Annual)
Agricultural Finance Statistics (Annual)

Other Reports (Continued)

Changes in Farm Production & Efficiency (Annual)
Farm Index (Monthly)
Foreign Agricultural Trade of the United States (Monthly)
Handbook of Agricultural Charts (Annual)
Livestock Feed Relationships—National & Geographic Areas (Annual)
National Food Review (Quarterly)
Price Spreads for Farm Foods (Monthly)
World Economic Conditions in Relation to Agricultural Trade (May, Nov.)

Commodity Futures Trading Commission

233 S. Wacker Dr., 46th Floor, Chicago, IL 60606

Commitments of Traders in Commodity Futures, with Market Concentration Ratios (M)

Superintendent of Documents

U.S. Government Printing Office, Washington, DC 20402

Construction Review (M) Catalog No. C57,509
Economic Indicators (M) Catalog No. Y4.Ec7
Foreign Agriculture, Including Foreign Crops & Markets (W) Catalog No. A67.7/2
Housing Starts (Construction Reports C.20) (M) Catalog No. C3.215/2
Statistical Abstract of the United States (A)
Survey of Current Business (M) Catalog No. C59.109
Treasury Bulletin (M) Catalog No. T1.3
Weekly Business Statistics (W) Catalog No. C56.109/2

U.S. Department of Agriculture. Forest Service

Washington, DC 20250

The Demand & Price Situation for Forest Products (A)
Forest Survey Reports
National Assessment of Timber Supply and Demand (every 10 years)
Production, Prices, Employment and Trade in Northwest Forest Industries (Q) Forest Service, Agriculture Dept., 319 SW Pine St., Portland, OR 97204

U.S. Department of Commerce. Bureau of the Census

Suitland, MD 20233

Business Conditions Digest (M)
Current Industrial Reports

U.S. Department of Interior. Bureau of Mines

Washington, DC 20241

Copper Production (M)
Gold & Silver (M)
Platinum (Q)

GLOSSARY

ACTUALS: The physical or cash commodity, as distinguished from commodity futures contracts.

ARBITRAGE: Simultaneous purchase of cash commodities or futures in the same or a different market, in order to profit from a discrepancy in prices. Also includes some aspects of "hedging."

BASIS: The difference between the spot or cash price of a commodity and the futures price of the same commodity. Basis is usually computed to the nearby futures contract, and may represent different time periods, product forms, qualities and locations.

BEAR: One who expects a decline in prices. The opposite of a "bull." A news item is considered bearish if it is expected to bring lower prices.

BID: An offer to buy a specific quantity of a commodity at a stated price.

BOARD ORDER or **MARKET IF TOUCHED** (MIT) **ORDER:** An order that becomes a market order when a particular price is reached. A sell MIT is placed above the market; a buy MIT is placed below the market.

BROKER: A person paid a fee or commission for executing buy or sell orders of a customer. In commodity futures trading, the term may refer to (1) *Floor Broker*—a person who actually executes orders on the trading floor of an exchange; (2) *Account Executive, Associated Person, Registered Commodity Representative*—the person who deals with customers in the offices of futures commission merchants; and (3) the *Futures Commission Merchant.*

BULL: One who expects a rise in prices. The opposite of a "bear." A news item is considered bullish if it portends higher prices.

CARRYING CHARGES: Cost of storing a physical commodity over a period of time. Includes insurance, storage, and interest on the invested funds as well as other incidental costs. It is a carrying charge market when there are higher futures prices for each successive contract month. If the carrying charge is adequate to reimburse the holder, it is called a full carrying charge.

CASH COMMODITY: The physical or actual commodity as distinguished from the futures. Sometimes called spot commodity or actuals.

CASH MARKET: A market for immediate delivery of and payment for cash commodities.

CASH PRICE: The price in the marketplace for actual cash or spot commodities to be delivered via customary market channels.

CHARTING: The use of graphs and charts in the technical analysis of futures markets to plot trends of price movements, average movements of price, and volume and open interest.

CHURNING: Excessive trading which permits the broker to derive a profit in commissions while disregarding the best interests of the customer.

CLEARING: The procedure through which the clearing house or association of a futures exchange becomes buyer to each seller of a futures contract, and seller to each buyer, on a daily basis, assuming responsibility for protecting buyers and sellers from financial loss by assuring performance on each contract.

CLOSE, THE: The period at the end of the trading session officially designated by the exchange during which all transactions are considered made "at the close."

COMMODITY FUTURES TRADING COMMISSION (CFTC): The Federal regulatory agency established by the CFTC Act of 1974 to administer the Commodity Exchange Act and to generally oversee the operations of the futures industry.

CONTRACT MONTH: The month in which delivery is to be made in accordance with a futures contract.

COVER: (1) Purchasing futures to offset a short position; (2) to have in hand the physical cash commodity when a short futures sale is made, or to acquire the commodity that might be deliverable on a short sale.

DAY TRADING: Establishing and offsetting the same futures market position within the time of a single trading session or day.

DEPOSITORY or **WAREHOUSE RECEIPT:** A document issued by a bank, warehouse, or other depository indicating ownership of a stored commodity. In the case of many commodities deliverable against futures contracts, transfer or ownership of an appropriate depository receipt may affect contract delivery.

DISCRETIONARY ACCOUNT: An arrangement by which the customer holding a commodity trading account gives written power of attorney to someone else, often the broker, to buy and sell commodity futures contracts without the prior approval of the customer. Often referred to as a "managed account."

EXPIRATION DATE: The date on which a particular commodity futures contract month expires; the last day of trading in that future.

FINANCIAL INSTRUMENT: Commodities which are themselves investment vehicles. Currency, securities, and indices of their value. Examples include shares, mortgages, commercial paper, Treasury Bills and Treasury Bonds.

FIRST NOTICE DAY: The first day on which notices of intention to deliver actual commodities against futures market positions can be received. First notice day will vary with each commodity and exchange.

FLOOR BROKER: Any person who, in or surrounding any pit or ring or other place provided by a contract market for the meeting of persons similarly engaged, executes for another any orders for the purchase or sale of any commodity for future delivery.

FLOOR TRADER: An exchange member who usually executes his or her own trades by being personally present in the pit. Sometimes called a "local."

FUNDAMENTAL ANALYSIS: Study of basic, underlying factors which will affect the supply and demand of the commodity being traded in futures contracts. Such factors are themselves called "the fundamentals."

FUTURES: A term used to designate the standardized contracts covering the sale of commodities for future delivery on a commodity exchange.

FUTURES CONTRACT: A firm commitment to deliver or to receive a specified quantity and grade of a commodity during the designated month with price being determined by public auction among exchange members.

FUTURES PRICE: The price of a given commodity unit determined at public auction by open outcry on a futures exchange.

HEDGING: Taking a positon in a futures market opposite to a position held in the cash market to minimize the risk of financial loss from an adverse price change; a purchase or sale of futures as a temporary substitute for a cash transaction that will occur later.

INTEREST RATE FUTURES: Futures contracts traded on commodities such as GNMA's, issuances of the U.S. Treasury, or commercial paper, the value of which is determined by interest rates and current yields. Currency is excluded from this category because interest rates play a much smaller role in the determination of currency values. Prices for interest rate futures generally move **inversely** in relation to interest rates. For example, when interest rates go up, the price on a financial instrument issued at a lower interest rate will have to be lowered to increase its yield to current levels.

INVERTED MARKET: A futures market in which the nearer months are selling at prices higher than the more distant months; hence a market displaying "inverse carrying charges," characteristic of markets in which supplies are currently short.

LIMIT ORDER: An order in which the customer sets a limit on price or other condition, such as time of an order, as contrasted with a "market order" which should be filled as soon as possible without pre-conditions.

LIMIT MOVE: A price that has advanced or declined the permissable limit allowed during one trading session, as fixed by the rules of a contract market. Limit moves may make execution of a customer's order impossible.

LIQUID MARKET: A market where large numbers of both buyers and sellers make order execution relatively simple, with minimal price changes.

LIQUIDATION: Making a transaction that offsets or closes out a long futures position.

LONG: (1) One who has bought a futures contract to establish a market position; (2) a market position which obligates the holder to take delivery; (3) one who owns an inventory of the cash commodity.

MARGIN: The amount of money or collateral deposited by a client with the broker, or by a broker with the clearinghouse, for the purpose of insuring the broker or clearinghouse against loss on open futures contracts. (1) *Original or initial margin* is the total amount of margin per contract required by the broker when a futures position is opened; (2) *Maintenance margin* is a sum which must be maintained on deposit at all times. If a customer's equity in any futures position drops to or under the level because of adverse price action, the broker must issue a margin call to restore the customer's equity.

MARGIN CALL: (1) A request from a brokerage firm to a customer to bring margin deposits up to minimum levels; (2) a request by the clearinghouse to a clearing member to bring clearing margins back to minimum levels required by the clearinghouse rules.

MARKET ORDER: An order to buy or sell a futures contract at whatever price is obtainable at the time it is entered in the ring or pit.

MINIMUM PRICE FLUCTUATION: Smallest increment of price movement possible in trading a given contract.

NEARBYS: The nearest delivery months of a commodity futures market. The contract month closest to expiration in any given commodity is the nearby contract.

OFFER: An indication of willingness to sell at a given price; opposite of "bid."

OFFSET: Liquidating a purchase of futures through the sale of an equal number of contracts of the same delivery month, or the covering of a short sale of futures through the purchase of an equal number of contracts of the same delivery month.

OPEN INTEREST: The sum of futures contracts in one delivery month or one market that has been entered into and not yet liquidated by offsetting transactions nor fulfilled by deliveries.

OPENING, THE: The period at the beginning of the trading session officially designated by the exchange during which all transactions are considered made "at the opening."

PAPER PROFIT: The profit that would be realized if the open contracts were liquidated as of a certain time or at a certain price.

PIT: A specially constructed arena on the trading floor of some exchanges where trading in a futures contract is conducted. On other exchanges, the term "ring" may designate the trading area for a commodity.

POSITION: An interest in the market, either long or short, in the form of one or more open contracts. The purchase of a contract would enter a "long" position; the sale of a contract would enter a "short" position.

POSITION LIMIT: The maximum position, either net long or net short, in one commodity future or in all futures of one commodity combined which may be held or controlled by one person as prescribed by an exchange or by the CFTC.

RANGE: The difference between the high and low price of a commodity during a given period fo time.

REALIZING: Accepting a profit or loss by liquidation or covering of an established futures position.

REPORTING LEVEL or **LIMIT:** Sizes of positions set by the exchanges and/or the CFTC at or above which commodity traders and brokers who carry their accounts must make daily reports as to the size of the positions by commodity, by delivery month, and whether the position is speculative or hedging.

RESTING ORDER: An order to buy at a price below or sell at a price above the prevailing market that is being held by a floor broker.

ROUND TURN: A completed transaction involving both a purchase and a liquidating sale, or a sale followed by a covering purchase. Commissions charged by brokers in commodity futures are charged only at the completion of the round turn.

SCALE DOWN (or **UP**): To purchase or sell on scale down means to buy or sell at regular price intervals in a declining market. To buy or sell on scale up means to buy or sell at regular price intervals as the market advances.

SETTLEMENT or **SETTLING PRICE:** The daily price at which the clearing house clears all trades and settles all accounts between clearing members for each contract month. The settlement price is established daily at the close of the trading session, after which all trades must be cleared before the next day's session. Settlement prices are used to determine both margin calls and invoice prices for deliveries.

SPOT: Market of immediate delivery of the product and immediate payment. Also may be used to refer to the nearest delivery month in futures.

STOP ORDER: An order that becomes a market order when a particular, stipulated price level is reached. A sell stop is placed below the current market; a buy stop is placed above the current market. The stop order may also be used as a "stop-loss" order.

STOP LIMIT ORDER: Like the stop order, this order goes into force only when there has been a trade somewhere in the pit at the stipulated price level. But the stop limit order, however, can only be filled at the stop limit price or better.

TECHNICAL ANALYSIS: An approach to analysis of futures markets and likely futures trends of commodity prices which examines patterns of price change, rates of change, and changes in volume and open interest. This data is often charted.

TENDER: The act of giving notice to the clearing house of intention to initiate delivery of the physical commodity in satisfaction of the futures contract.

TRADING LIMIT: (1) The maximum quantity of a commodity future which may be purchased or sold by one person during one trading day; (2) The maximum futures position any individual is allowed to hold at any time under CFTC regulation; (3) The price above or below which trading is not allowed during any one day.

VOLUME OF TRADE: The number of contracts traded during a specified period of time. It may be quoted as the number of contracts traded or in total of physical units. Note that volume is **not** the same as open interest.